Knot Tying for Kids

A Fun and Easy Guide to Mastering Essential Knots for Young Adventurers

© Copyright 2024 - All rights reserved.

The content contained within this book may not be reproduced, duplicated, or transmitted without direct written permission from the author or the publisher.

Under no circumstances will any blame or legal responsibility be held against the publisher or author for any damages, reparation, or monetary loss due to the information contained within this book, either directly or indirectly.

Legal Notice:

This book is copyright-protected. It is only for personal use. You cannot amend, distribute, sell, use, quote, or paraphrase any part of the content within this book without the consent of the author or publisher.

Disclaimer Notice:

Please note the information contained within this document is for educational and entertainment purposes only. All effort has been executed to present accurate, up-to-date, reliable, and complete information. No warranties of any kind are declared or implied. Readers acknowledge that the author is not engaging in the rendering of legal, financial, medical, or professional advice. The content within this book has been derived from various sources. Please consult a licensed professional before attempting any techniques outlined in this book.

By reading this document, the reader agrees that under no circumstances is the author responsible for any losses, direct or indirect, that are incurred as a result of the use of the information contained within this document, including, but not limited to, errors, omissions, or inaccuracies.

Table of Contents

INTRODUCTION LETTER TO PARENTS 1
INTRODUCTION LETTER TO CHILDREN 3
SECTION 1: KNOTS IN HISTORY 5
SECTION 2: GETTING STARTED 30
SECTION 3: BASIC KNOTS 36
SECTION 4: NAUTICAL KNOTS 46
SECTION 5: KNOTS FOR OUTDOOR ADVENTURES 52
SECTION 6: EVERYDAY KNOTS 77
SECTION 7: KNOTTING FOR FUN 93
SECTION 8: TIPS AND TRICKS 108
THANK YOU 116
REFERENCES 117

Introduction Letter to Parents

Dear Parents,

    Every parent's and guardian's dream is to see their children grow up to become independent and self-sufficient adults. For this to happen, children must learn numerous essential skills that will help them navigate through the complexities of life. Knot tying is fun – but also a handy skill that teaches children problem solving, memorization, and critical thinking.

    While mastering knot tying is often recommended for outdoor adventurers, your child can benefit from it even if they aren't interested in exploring the wilderness. They can incorporate this skill into a fun hobby or simply use it to navigate everyday life more efficiently. They can save themselves a lot of time and trouble by mastering basic everyday knots (like shoe laces), advanced knots if they wish to help with the boat, and various creative projects to pass the time – without a screen! This book has all the tools to help them do that.

    Knot tying is challenging; some children will take more time to learn it, but this book will ensure they'll get there. Don't worry if your child didn't acquire this or similar skills through traditional means before; perhaps they just had trouble paying attention to intricate or tedious instructions. With easy-to-follow practical steps, this book is designed to guide young learners through the knot-tying process regardless of their abilities or experience level.

    Help your child get started learning knot-tying safely and responsibly. There are some safety rules in the beginning chapters, providing a head start in helping you be the supportive parent your child needs as they embark on their knot-tying journey.

Have fun!

Introduction Letter to Children

Hey there!

Did you know that knot-tying has been used for centuries – and not just for securing things. While tying a secure knot does come in handy in everyday situations, like preventing your shoelaces from becoming untied, knots can also have many other purposes. From ceremonial functions to art to hunting and fishing, knot tying has played a central part in the lives of different cultures and civilizations since ancient times. If you love exploring the great outdoors, you'll find this skill particularly handy as it can help you remain safe and resolve any issues that might come up during your adventures.

Knot tying can also be a fun activity you might enjoy during your free time. Plenty of arts and crafts require knots for completing or creating projects. You can use knots to express whatever you feel or think, just like you would use drawing, coloring, or any other art form. Not only that, you'll learn other skills along the way, like being resourceful in tricky situations and solving seemingly insurmountable problems.

Whatever draws you to knot tying, you're about to find the gateway to exciting discoveries in the world of knots and your own abilities. Mastering this skill will teach you much about yourself, including your likes and dislikes and strengths and weaknesses. It will also help you work on those strengths or weaknesses and be more confident in navigating the world around you. You'll learn patience and the value of hard work, but **FUN** work!

If you're ready to embark on this exciting journey into the world of knot-tying, you can start by reading the first chapter!

Section 1: Knots in History

When you think of knots, you probably think of tying your shoelaces or knots sailors use on boats. While these might be the most universal uses for knot tying, the art has been around for thousands of years, and knots have been used for many other purposes throughout the centuries. Knots, created by tying a piece of string, cord, or rope, have evolved from simple fastenings for everyday objects to complex structures for arts and crafts projects.

Often, finding a new purpose for a knot tie led to the discovery of new uses for universal objects or the invention of other objects. Nowadays, you can tie a knot virtually in infinite ways, depending on what you'll be using it for. By reading this section, you'll learn how knot tying was featured across history and how important this skill was in different cultures.

Knot tying is an art that has been around for thousands of years.
https://pixabay.com/photos/flower-lis-knot-darling-rope-1934110/

An Ancient Tool

The earliest evidence of people using knots coincides with the use of primitive tools. We believe humans have used ropes for at least 15,000-17,000 years; this is an estimate – historians think the use of ropes could possibly even predate the invention of fire! Other tools, like the axe and wheels, were invented much later, and rope tying played a crucial role in their creation. The first axes were simple stone heads tied to wood handles.

Somewhere between 8,000 and 6,500 BC, people began to create textile fabrics for clothes and other purposes. They tied and secured the different pieces of material with knots. As the civilizations developed further, so did the use of knots and rope to create other devices and structures. Some of the first mechanisms knots were used for were fishing and hunting traps.

Around 4,000 BC, the Egyptians invented a *spindle*, which made creating ropes much easier. By the third century BC, Roman warriors went into battle armed with sling bolts they made from ropes tied into knots.

Jumping a little farther ahead in history to 1,200 AD, the Arab nations were creating knots to secure their garments and household textiles and decorate them. As sea travel picked up, so did the import of this knot-tying art. Soon, the Europeans were using it to adorn their clothes.

By this time in history, knot tying grew from creating simple knots (like the *overhand knot* you would use for tying off the end of something) to numerous complicated knots. Ancient civilizations alone came up with 19 different knots, including the bowline, the bottle sling, the clove hitch, the cat's paw, the Eskimo bowline, the fishermen and the double fishermen, the figure-eight, the overhand, the running bowline, the thief, the reef, and the Turks head knots, along with the Kalmyk loop, the single and half hitch, the two half hitches, the overhand loop, and the one-sided overhand bend. Below are instructions to some of these knots.

Bottle Sling

Instructions:

1. Take a one-foot-long piece of string and fold it in half.
2. Lay the folded string down flat with the two sides parallel to each other. The loop should be at the top and the two open ends at the bottom.
3. Find the third of the folded string length from the top (the loop) and fold it downward. The loop should lie on top of the parallel strings, creating two "ears".
4. Twist both "ears" towards you and then back down, creating a small twist at their bottom.
5. Put the left "ear" over the right one, and under them, you'll find a small hole.
6. Put your fingers in the hole, and pull it downwards until you make it into a larger, loop.
7. Take this third loop at the bottom, bring it up, and pull it through the other two loops on the top.
8. Pull the third loop upwards, and the other two downwards. The double loop at the bottom goes over a bottleneck.
9. Once you put the double loop on the bottle, you can pull the third loop and the two ends of the string to tighten the loop around the bottle.
10. Tie the strings free ends off, and you'll be left with two small handles on the bottleneck to lift and carry the bottle.

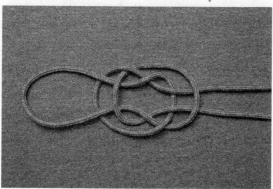

Bottle sling.

David J. Fred, CC BY-SA 3.0 <https://creativecommons.org/licenses/by-sa/3.0>, via Wikimedia Commons. https://commons.wikimedia.org/wiki/File:Bottle_Sling_ABOK_1142_Tying_Complete.jpg

Cat's Paw on a Ring
Instructions:
1. Make a loop with your rope and pull it over a ring. The loop should be behind the two strands.
2. Pull the two ends of the rope through the loop.
3. Make the loop in the middle larger by pulling it downwards.
4. Turn the ring away from yourself, into the loop again, and then around, away from yourself.
5. Pull the rope's ends downward while adjusting the loop to tighten it.
6. Work toward the ring until you get a tight knot that looks like a cat's paw underneath it.
7. It makes a nice keychain.

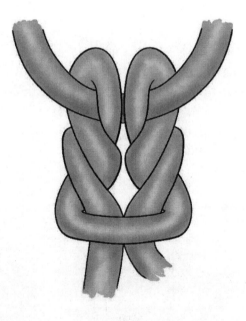

Cat's Paw on a Ring

Eskimo Bowline
Instructions:
1. Lay a piece of string flat and create a loop underneath it by tossing the right end to the left, and then to the right. You've created an overhand loop
2. Take the left end of the string, and place it straight underneath the loop.
3. Take the same end and pull it over the loop, thread it under the straight line you've created in the previous step.
4. Pull the end over the left side of the loop.
5. Grab the loop with your left hand, and the longer end of the rope with your right hand, and gently pull the knot tight. The knot will look similar to a regular bowline except its tied around part of the loop.
6. You can use the Eskimo bowline anytime you want a secure knot in a place where a regular knot can come loose, like tightening equipment when climbing and hiking.

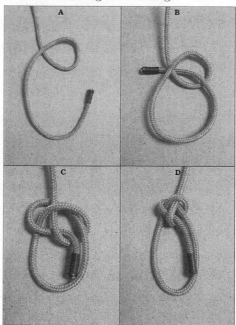

Eskimo Bowline.
FFouche, CC BY-SA 4.0 <https://creativecommons.org/licenses/by-sa/4.0>, via Wikimedia Commons. https://commons.wikimedia.org/wiki/File:Eskimo_Boeglynknoop.jpg

Running Bowline

Instructions:

1. Loop the rope around a pen.
2. Create a bight and pass one of the ropes end over the other. The bight should be under the crossing point of the two ends
3. Thread the rope under the second (non-working) end and through the loop.
4. Pull the working end behind the loop around the pole.
5. Thread it back through the loop
6. Tighten by pulling the ends toward the left.
7. The finished knot is similar to a regular bowline with an extra loop added to it before its tied. Its useful when you want to throw a loop over something you want to catch.

Running bowline.
Malta, CC BY-SA 2.5 <https://creativecommons.org/licenses/by-sa/2.5>, via Wikimedia Commons. https://commons.wikimedia.org/wiki/File:N%C5%93ud_de_laguis.jpg

The Thief
Instructions:
1. Make a bight (loop) at one end of the rope
2. Feed the opposite end of the rope through the loop from under the loop.
3. Pulling this end over the top, loop it back underneath the first loop. After you make the second loop, put the end of the rope on top of it — the two ends of the rope should look in opposite directions.
4. Thread the end of the right side under the loop, and pull both ends tight to finish off the knot.
5. The finished thief knot look like a square knot, except that the loose ends are on the opposite ends of the knot. Its often used to close bags.

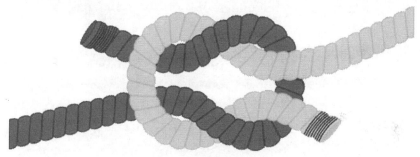

The thief.

SuperManu, CC BY-SA 3.0 <https://creativecommons.org/licenses/by-sa/3.0>, via Wikimedia Commons. https://commons.wikimedia.org/wiki/File:Thief_knot_noeud_de_voleur.svg

Turks Head Knot
Instructions:
1. Fold a piece of paracord in half over a pen.
2. Make a circle around the pen with the paracord by bringing the two ends together and folding them in opposite directions.
3. Pass the left-hand end underneath the right-hand one.
4. Again, pass the left-hand strand and over it over the first loop.
5. Pass the working end underneath the right-hand end.
6. Place the right-hand end over the second loop and pass it under the first loop.
7. Turn over the pen and pass the top loop over the bottom loop.
8. Move the end on the bottom over the bottom loop and under the top loop.
9. Thread the top end under the top loop and pass it over the bottom loop.
10. Pull the knot tight. Once you remove it from a pen the knot has a circular shape. You can use it as a decoration at the end of the pen or any circular object you use.

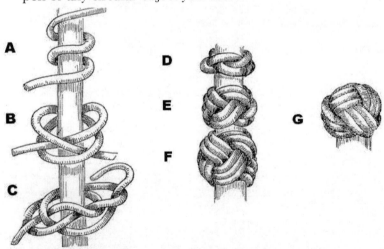

Turks head knot.
https://commons.wikimedia.org/wiki/File:Turks_head.png

The Kalmyk Loop
Instructions:
1. Form a small loop with your string.
2. Pass one end of the string over the top of the loop and pull it under. You now have an inner loop on the left and an outer loop on the right side.
3. From the leftover end on the same side, create a bight (fold the string in half), and pass it over the outer loop and under and up over the inner loop (the original one).
4. Pull the large loop you've created on the right side to tighten the knot.
5. Its similar to the Eskimo bowline, except its tied with a bight, but can be used for the same purposes.

The Kalmyk Loop.
Obersachse, CC BY-SA 4.0 <https://creativecommons.org/licenses/by-sa/4.0>, via Wikimedia Commons. https://commons.wikimedia.org/wiki/File:Kalm%C3%BCckenknoten.jpg

You'll learn about the rest of the knots soon.

Knot tying was also featured in Chinese knotting, made popular by the Tang and Song Dynasties between the 10th and the 13th centuries. By this time, Chinese folk artists used 11 types of knots, including the good luck, the four-flower, the cross, , the double connection, the Chinese button, the double coin, the square, the Pan Chang, the Agemaki, and the Plafond knot. Below are instructions to some of these knots.

Good Luck Knot

Instructions:

1. Fold your cord in half and lay it flat. Pin the top loop down.
2. About four inches from the top of the loop on the right side, form another loop (bight). Pin it down.
3. Repeat step 2 on the left side.
4. Take the loose ends from the bottom and fold them over the left loop. They should be parallel to the top loop, and you should have a small to the bottom left from the center.
5. Move the left loop over the loose ends and the top loop. It should lay around half of the right loop.
6. Move the top loop over the loops on the right.
7. Thread the longer right loop over the small hole from step 4.
8. Tighten the knot by gently tugging on both ends and the loops until you have a square shape at the center.
9. Move the left loop over the bottom one, leaving a small opening between them.
10. Move the bottom loop over the two right loops and onto the right side of the ends.
11. Move the strands over the left loop and thread them through the small opening from step 9.
12. Tighten the loop to create a middle square made of the four quarters. There should be tiny loops on the edges of all quarters and three loops coming from left, right, and top of the square.

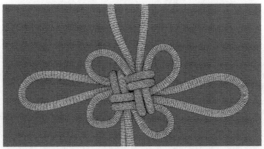

Good luck knot.
Zaripov Rustem, CC BY-SA 4.0 <https://creativecommons.org/licenses/by-sa/4.0>, via Wikimedia Commons.
https://commons.wikimedia.org/wiki/File:Good_luck_knot(ABOK_2437).jpg

Four-Flower Knot
Instructions:
1. Take two cords and fold both to create two loops. Cross the loop of the second cord over the loop of the first one.
2. Fold the second loop down and throw the loose strands of the second cord over it to make a knot.
3. You now have one loop and four strands coming from it. Pin the loop down.
4. Pass the third strand over the fourth one, then bring it back from under, creating a knot on the fourth strand.
5. Repeat step 4.
6. Repeat steps 4 and 5 on the other side by passing the second strand over and under the first one two times.
7. Double up the first and fourth strands to make a loop.
8. Thread the third strand through the loop from the previous step and do the same with the second strand.
9. Gently pull all four ends tight. You'll have four small flower shapes in the middle. You can use it for decorations.

Four-Flower Knot.

Cross

Instructions:

1. Make a loop with your cord.
2. Place the left strand behind the right one to create a second loop on the left, then move the left strand back to the left side to make a third loop on the right.
3. Feed the right strand through the top loop from under. Then, feed it through the right-hand loop from over.
4. Tighten by adjusting the strands.
5. The finished knot has a cross shape on both sides (front and back). Can be used for decorations or tying a tie.

Cross knot.

BougeToi, CC BY-SA 4.0 <https://creativecommons.org/licenses/by-sa/4.0>, via Wikimedia Commons. https://commons.wikimedia.org/wiki/File:Chinese_Cross_knot_front_view.jpg

Double Connection (Double Happiness)
Instructions:
1. Fold your cord and lay the two strands horizontally.
2. Pass the bottom strand over the top one and bring it down under to form a loop.
3. Move the same strand back over the loop you've just created.
4. Close the loop by tightening the strands.
5. Use the other strand to make a loop over the first strand (under the knot you've made in step 4).
6. Then, thread the second strand through the first loop and the one made in the previous step.
7. Tuck on both loops slowly to close the two loops until you get a cross shape in the middle.
8. Often used in ceremonies to celebrate a connection between two people.

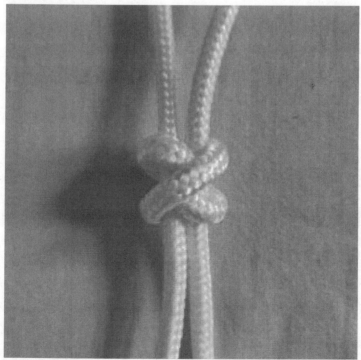

Double Connection.
BougeToi, CC BY-SA 4.0 <https://creativecommons.org/licenses/by-sa/4.0>, via Wikimedia Commons. https://commons.wikimedia.org/wiki/File:Chinese_Double_Connection_knot.jpg

Pan Chang
Instructions:
1. Prepare a piece of paracord, pins, and a Styrofoam pad (or a similar surface into which you can put your pins).
2. Fold the cord by leaving a little more cord on the left end. You create a bight facing up. Pin it down on the top of the loop.
3. Using the right end of the cord, make a second bight — this one should be facing down.
4. Pin it down, make a third bight on the left end) also facing down) and pin this one as well)
5. Take the right end of the cord, make a bight, and feed this bight first under the outer line, then over the inner line of the second bight (the one you created in step 2.). Continue threading it under the outer line and over the inner line of the original bite.
6. Repeat step 5 to create two horizontal bights. Pin both on the right side.
7. Pin the small squares in the middle and the cords right end.
8. Take the cord's left end threading through the small loop on the top right, under the next four lines, and bring it out at the left side again.
9. Repeat the previous step in the middle (the space between the two horizontal bights from step 6).
10. Thread the cord's left end under the through the opening on the bottom left. Moving upwards on the left side, cross the end over the next three lines, under the next two.
11. Turning back downwards, pass the end through the top left loop, under the next two lines, under one line, under the next three, over one, and finally under the last line to emerge at the bottom.
12. Repeat steps 10 and 11 in the middle (between two vertical bights).
13. Remove the pins and slowly tighten the knot by adjusting the loops one by one.
14. You'll have a flat square knot made of lots of tiny knots. You can use if for decoration, necklaces, key chains, etc.

Pan Chang.
Zaripov Rustem, CC BY-SA 4.0 <https://creativecommons.org/licenses/by-sa/4.0>, via Wikimedia Commons. https://commons.wikimedia.org/wiki/File:Pan_chang.png

Agemaki

Instructions:

1. Take a 3-foot-long cord, take one end, and thread it under and over the top to create an overhand knot.
2. Thread the other hand of the cord through the knot and make another overhand knot. The two knots should be next to each other.
3. Take the inner side of the left knot and pull it through the right knot. At the same time, take the inner side of the right knot and pull it through the left one.
4. You'll have three loops (left, top, and right), and the loose ends on the bottom. Gently pull on all these, adjusting them until you've tightened the intricate Agemaki knot in the middle. The finished knot looks like a dragonfly.
5. Traditionally the knot was used on Samurai armor, but it can be used as a decoration too.

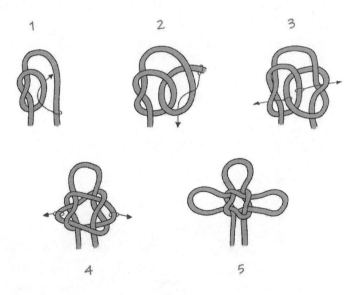

Agemaki.

True Lover's Knot

Instructions:

1. Create an overhand loop.
2. Tuck the working end under the loop and pull it on the top. Tighten it a little bit to create a simple overhand knot.
3. Using the working end of the rope, create another loop over the first one.
4. Thread the rope'
5. s end under the original loop, then loop it back toward the top to create a third loop.
6. Tuck the working end through the third loop to create a second overhand knot.
7. Tighten the right overhand knot first, then tighten the left one as well to finish the true love knot.
8. It looks similar to a square knot (except the strands face different directions) and is used for decorations.

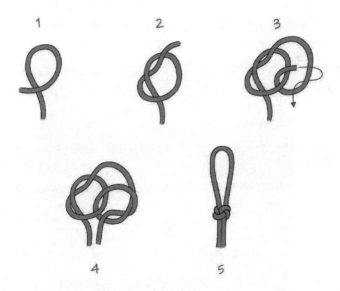

True Lover's Knot.

Plafond Knot

Instructions:

1. Make a loop, then thread one of the strands over it to make a half knot.
2. Make a second half knot under the first one. Tighten this one a little, but leave the first loop big.
3. Leave some space under the second half knot, make a loop, and convert it into a third half knot.
4. Make a fourth half knot under and fold the part with the last two half knots into the middle part.
5. Fold the upper loop on top of the center.
6. Take the top of the upper loop (bight) and feed it through the bottom half knots (the actual knots, not the loops).
7. Feed the left strand through the top two half knots.
8. Thread the right strand through the first strand in the middle, then through the top half knots.
9. Pull on two loose strands and the loop at the top to tighten the knot. You can place it at the end of zippers for decorations and to make move the zipper up and down easier.

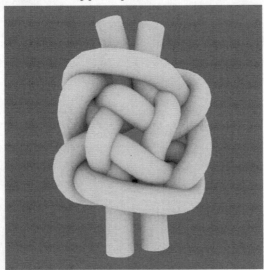

Plafond knot.
Zaripov Rustem, CC BY-SA 4.0 <https://creativecommons.org/licenses/by-sa/4.0>, via Wikimedia Commons. https://commons.wikimedia.org/wiki/File:Plafond_knot.png

You'll learn about the rest later.

In the late 15th century, Europeans discovered another use for knot tying. These were ropewalks . . . long and narrow structures between which they could twist rope and create different forms of knots. During the 15th century, the Incas used knot-tying for recordkeeping. They recorded their calendars and important events in a complex textile system called *Khipu* (or *quipu*), made by intricate knotting.

By the 17th century, knot-tying for different purposes was widespread in Europe, so it's no surprise that it made its way to the courts, too. Macramé was invented, and Queen Mary the Second and her ladies-in-waiting spent much of their time making different decorations through this unique art form.

Knot tying kept evolving as people kept finding ways to create new knots. Whenever they thought there were no more ways to tie something into a knot, they added another twist or loop and ended up with a new and often more complex structure.

The Revolution of Knot Tying

One of the biggest discoveries in knot tying was using knots in sailboats. Knots were used in many different ways on boats, including for rigging, a system that sailors used to control their vessels. While primitive knots had been used on boats beforehand, the practice truly picked up in the early 19th century, when new uses were invented. Around this time, people started transporting everything by boat, including large objects and animals (as there were no planes, trains, or cars). Tying up the cargo allowed sailors to secure it and prevent it from moving due to a strong tide (or distraction in the case of animals). They would simply tie the knot at the end of the rope they used to secure the items or animals, and they could travel safely. One of the most commonly used knots for this purpose was the bowline knot, a tying form presumably invented by the ancient Egyptians.

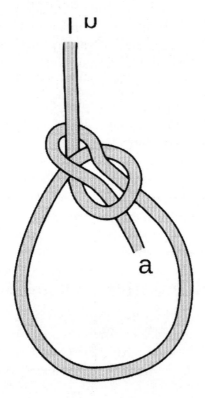

The bowline knot is a tying form presumably invented by the ancient Egyptians. Helladerivative work: Tescobar, CC BY-SA 2.5 <https://creativecommons.org/licenses/by-sa/2.5>, via Wikimedia Commons: https://commons.wikimedia.org/wiki/File:Bowline_(standard).svg

Sailors and remarkable knot crafters often developed new, more secure structures – many of which are still used today, not just on boats but on other outdoor adventures.

Besides continually inventing new knots to secure things on their ships, sailors also practiced an artistic knotwork called cox-combing. While the main purpose of this knotwork was to decorate the ship, it also served as protection. Some sailors also used coxcomb patterns to identify their ships. Some commonly used cox-combing knots were the Flemish, the French whipping, and the Turk's head knots. While the practice isn't as common as it once was, some modern boaters still place similar knotwork on their rudders, tillers, and wheels.

Sailors also invented the measurement called a knot (known as the sailor's knot today), using it to gauge how fast their ship traveled across the water. They measured this with a device that consisted of a pie-shaped piece of wood and a rope coil with regularly spaced knots across it. By lowering the wood piece into the water, they could track how much of the rope was unraveling during a specific time. When this time passed, they would pull in the rope and count the number of knots on the part that unraveled. The number of knots gave them the boat's speed.

Modern Uses for Knots

While knot use on ships and boats isn't as popular as it was when these vessels were the main transportation methods people used to get around (mainly because modern ships are powered by steam engines and not wind through sails), knot tying has found its way into many other areas of life.

Besides using them in recreational sailing and other outdoor adventures, you may have already encountered a few examples of knot-tying without even realizing it. For example, have you ever seen someone tie a necktie or make a knitted sweater? Even sewn pieces of cloth can have elements that require tying together or serving as decorations.

Basket weavers and rug knitters also use knot tying to create their pieces. Girls with long hair often wear intricate braids, which can include knots. And, if you're an outdoor adventurer, you've probably encountered (or will in the future) many different types of knots as they are used for securing equipment during camping, fishing, mountaineering, rock climbing, hiking, and many other purposes.

Beyond making the trip more enjoyable, knowing how to secure a knot can be a lifesaver during wilderness adventures. You may need knots to attach ropes together so you and your equipment remain secure and avoid losing an essential piece you'll need later (like food, water, first-aid, camping equipment, flashlights, etc.).

Another popular use of knot tying is in macramé, which innovative crafters re-popularized in the 1970s. Some commonly used knots in macramé are the overhand knot (this one truly has many uses), the square knot, the clove hitch, the spiral stitch, and the Lark's head knot.

Spiral Stitch
Instructions:
1. Make two Lark's head knots with two separate strings on a pen.
2. Pass the first strand over the second and third strands and under the fourth strand.
3. Pass the fourth strand under the third and second strands and over the first strand.
4. Tighten the knot you've created, then repeat steps 2 and 3 on the same side several times. Your pattern will take a spiral form naturally.

Spiral stitch.

The other common macramé knots will be described later in the book.

Macramé pieces are typically fashioned with cotton rope, which comes in many colors. Just like in other uses, knot tying in macramé has expanded vastly. This way, all generations can enjoy it. Unlike its original version, which only included intricate designs, the modern version often has wooden or plastic beads, crystals, and other small objects added to it.

As you can see, knots are a versatile tool with numerous functions in people's lives. You can use them for essential functions as people have done since the beginning of time, in outdoor adventures, in crafty hobbies, or for other purposes – the choices are virtually limitless.

The Meaning of Knots in Different Cultures

Beyond practical or decorative purposes, knots have a distinctive meaning in different cultures across the globe.

Celtic Symbols

The Celtic knot is one of their most well-known emblems.
freepatternsarea, CC BY 4.0 <https://creativecommons.org/licenses/by/4.0>, via Wikimedia Commons: https://commons.wikimedia.org/wiki/File:Meaning_of_Celtic_Trinity_Knot_Symbol_and_Free_Template.jpg

The ancient Celts fondly used different symbols to express their religious beliefs, ideas, and discoveries. The Celtic knot is one of their most well-known emblems; it may be found in Celtic art and historical objects such as the Book of Kells, a text whose cover is decorated with elaborate knot work. The Celtic cross was also originally designed as a form of knot symbolizing the sun god.

Notable Celtic knots include the Triquetra, often known as the Trinity Knot. Its three distinct sections, representing the sacred sequence of threes in the Celtic culture, are created from one continuous line. The ancients believed that good things came in threes and tied the number to many things you'll see in nature, including the moon's phases.

Have you heard the phrase "tying the knot?" It's used when two people get married because, in ancient times, the bride and groom had their hands tied together as part of their wedding ceremony. This practice hails from the Celtic culture, where it was called handfasting (some still use these kinds of ceremonies today). The couple was asked to take each other's hand while a third person tied their hands with a cord or a ribbon so they would look like a knot. Different colors were used to symbolize what the couple promised to each other (for example, blue ribbons meant trust and devotion), much like newlyweds express this to each other in their vows.

Egyptian Symbolism

In ancient Egypt, knots were seen as a symbol of infinite paths and firm connections. Both symbols come from the Egyptian's reverence for their gods and goddesses. Different knots were used to represent the eternal life of deities in ceremonies held in their honor and to celebrate those with good values.

Chinese Symbolism

The Chinese used knots in weddings, and knotwork is still featured in modern ceremonies. *Ucla90024, CC BY-SA 3.0 <https://creativecommons.org/licenses/by-sa/3.0>, via Wikimedia Commons: https://commons.wikimedia.org/wiki/File:Chinese_Knot_P4R.jpg*

Like the ancient Celts, the Chinese also used knots in weddings, and knotwork is still featured in modern ceremonies. The double happiness and true love knots are still among the most often used knots in Chinese weddings. Couples can also gift artwork containing these knots to each other before their wedding.

In Chinese culture, knots (particularly the red ones) are seen as symbols of good fortune. In ancient times, if a Chinese family wanted to chase away bad luck from their lives, they would decorate their house with red-knotted artwork. They believed that by keeping misfortune away, they left room for good luck to come into their home. Other knots in Chinese culture are used for protection in dangerous situations or when they believe someone wants to cause harm to another. And just like they had knots for unity, the Chinese also used knotwork to represent freedom.

Section 2: Getting Started

Knot tying is a basic skill that anyone can learn. It may not seem like it, but you'll notice that there are many times when tying a knot is useful - for both fun and serious work. It helps to know about many kinds of knots and when to use them because you can quickly be thrown into the deep end, where you have to think on your feet. When the situation arises, and a skilled person who knows how to tie knots is called forward, you will be the savior who steps up and knows exactly what to do!

Knots are for the adventurer who spends a lot of time outdoors. Whether camping, fishing, or mountain climbing, not knowing much about knots may leave you struggling at the wrong moments. So, one of the first steps toward becoming a survival expert and a handy person is knowing the basics. Once you have mastered the basics, you can move on to more complicated knots to impress your friends and family. Get ready to jump into the incredible world of knot tying and unleash a whole new skill set that will help make you the coolest person in the woods - and anywhere a rope is around.

Knots are used on boats, as well as securing plants and trees.
https://pixabay.com/photos/knitting-rope-node-marine-2428151/

Beyond being outside, tying knots will help you in many situations around the house or on the road. For example, if you plan to move a lot of goods on a pick-up truck, it may be necessary to tie down the items so they don't fall off along the way. You might one day find yourself having to tow a friend who got stuck on the side of the road. Knowing a strong knot will ensure the car is safely secured.

Knots are often used in gardening to secure trees or various plants into position. Knots are used in construction to secure equipment, building materials, and boats. So, as you get older, you'll find more use for what you've learned in this book. Best to start learning now to stay ahead of the game and never be caught off guard by a tricky situation!

Basic Knot Tying Kit: Tools and Materials Needed for Knot Tying

Every adventure expert says a strong rope is super important to have in your backpack when you go hiking. Builders and mechanics also love ropes because they can do so many helpful things on the job or in a garage. Knowing about different ropes and tools makes you a cool knot-tying hero!

It's really smart to have a rope and knot-tying kit ready for emergencies. With a rope and some gadgets like hooks, clips, and pulleys, you can make awesome tools to help you out. Need to lift something heavy by yourself? A pulley can make it easy-peasy. Want to hang a hammock in the forest or keep your stuff safe from animals by tying it up in a tree? Or maybe you need to keep things tied down at a building site or fix something quickly at home. These are all times when your knot-tying kit comes in handy. You can carry your kit in a small bag or leave it in your family's car. With the right skills and gear, you'll be ready to solve any problem with a rope and your smart knot ideas.

Types of Rope

Ropes are super important for tying knots - the star of your knot-tying kit! You can skip some tools, but you definitely need rope because no rope means no knots. There are lots of different ropes for different tasks, and here's a quick guide to some of them:

- **Cotton Rope:** Good for gardening and decorating your room. It's nice to the planet, but it doesn't like getting wet because it gets heavier and can break easily.
- **Nylon Rope:** Outdoor adventurers love this one! It's super strong, bends well, and can carry heavy stuff without a sweat.
- **Manila Rope:** Made from plants, it's fantastic for garden work but doesn't like water too much - it shrinks and can break after a while.
- **Polypropylene Rope:** Builders and boat lovers use this because it's light, tough, and even floats on water.
- **Polyester Rope:** Really strong and doesn't stretch or mind the heat. Great for tying things down securely or for flagpoles.
- **HMPE Rope:** Superhero strong - even stronger than steel! Perfect for outdoor adventures because it ties really good knots.

Each type of rope has its own special job, so pick the right rope for your adventure or project!

Clip

Clips can either be made of plastic or metal. Specialized clips like carabiners are used in rock climbing. This versatile tool allows you to attach ropes to many different items in unique ways.

Pulley

A pulley is a wheel that a rope passes over. Pulleys help decrease the weight of items, and they can be used in different combinations to make lifting and moving heavy items easier.

Ring

Rings are simple metal circles that you can use to tie objects in different ways. The ring's simple design allows it to be used creatively in many scenarios and is a handy tool to keep with you.

Scissors

Sometimes, you must cut a rope shorter, or you may have no choice but to snip a tangled mess. A scissor is a simple tool everybody has around the house that can always be useful when tying knots or working with rope.

Cleat

A cleat is a T-shaped object usually made of wood or metal. This tool is secured to a flat surface for you to tie a rope around. You will see cleats at docks for people to tie their boats down.

Hook

A hook is a curved piece of metal used to hang objects on. Keeping some screw-in hooks nearby can be helpful in many situations where you need to secure something or hang objects on it.

Practical Applications of Knots

Knowing just one or two knots isn't enough because different adventures need different types of knots! Think about it: you use a knot daily to tie your shoes before heading out. Knots are super handy for tying things together, carrying heavy stuff, and keeping things in place.

Some knots are easy to untie when needed, and some are super strong and won't loosen up, no matter what. With all the knots you can learn, you'll always find the perfect one for what you're doing, whether you need to keep something tied tight or gently lower something heavy to the ground.

Knots are not just for one thing; they're used everywhere - from homes to the great outdoors – and even in all kinds of jobs. This book will make you a knot-tying champ, ready for any situation, whether you're by a lake, in the ocean, on land, building something, or out camping or hunting. Knots helped people build amazing things and are a super cool skill that's been a bit forgotten. But once you dive into the world of knots, you'll see how awesome and important they really are!

Basic Knot Terminology

When you start learning to tie knots, the instructions will use common words. Without understanding the meanings of these words, you could quickly become lost, causing a lot of unnecessary struggle. The words listed below will help you sound like you know what you are talking about and allow you to follow instructions correctly.

Bight

This describes the part of the rope that is between the two ends. It is mainly used to discuss any curved section on a rope that has not been tied.

Loop

Once two parts of your rope cross each other, the bight will now become a loop. A loop will either be overhand or underhand, depending on the positioning of your standing part. If the working end goes over your standing part, it is an *overhand* loop; if it goes under your standing part, it is an *underhand* loop.

Crossing Point

The crossing point is where two sections of your rope cross to form a loop.

Working End

The working end is the section of the rope you are handling to tie the knot.

Standing Part

The standing part is also known as the standing end. This is the end of the rope you are not actively using to tie a knot.

Practice, Practice, and Practice

When you first start tying knots, it will be difficult. You may have to keep looking over the instructions and moving slowly. The more you practice, the faster and better you will become! If you work on your rope-tying skills, you will be ready when the time comes to put them to use. It does not help just reading about different kinds of knots and their uses. You must get out there and get your hands dirty.

Test Your Skills and Knowledge

1. What is a *pulley*, and what can it be used for?
2. If you were making a rope-tying kit, which items would you include?
3. Why is it important to always carry a rope with you if you are going out into the wilderness?
4. List five uses of ropes you could see applied in your everyday life.
5. What is a "bight"?
6. What does the "loop" refer to when tying a knot?
7. What does "working end" refer to when tying a knot?
8. Which part of the rope is the *standing end* when tying a knot?
9. How can a pair of scissors be helpful when you need to tie a knot?
10. Name three types of ropes and their uses.

Section 3: Basic Knots

Now that you've picked up some cool knot words and what they're for, you're all set to start tying! Remember, learning to tie knots is like learning to walk before you can run. First up, we'll cover the basics. You might know some of these knots already, and some might be totally new to you. Start with these simple ones, and soon, you'll be ready for more tricky knots that use the same ideas.

Even though these first knots are for beginners, they're super useful in lots of different ways. You'll learn how to tie them and where - and why - they're handy. But don't stop there! Once you've got the hang of them, try your own ideas. Learning knots is all about getting creative with ropes and strings. So, if you think a knot could work somewhere else, go for it and try it out. These basics will help you see rope in a whole new way - not just as a piece of string but as an awesome tool for all kinds of tasks and fun.

Square knot.
https://commons.wikimedia.org/wiki/File:Platteknoop.svg

Square Knot

The square knot is one of the first techniques people learn because it is used for the laces on our shoes. The square knot is also known as a reef knot because it was once used to secure sails in rough winds. This knot works amazingly for tying bundles together, so it can be used both in the home and outdoors. The square knot has even been used to tie bandages tightly if the blood from a wound needs to be stopped quickly. This simple knot is easy to learn and can come in handy in many scenarios if you use your imagination.

How to Tie a Square Knot:

1. Grab hold of the two ends of a rope.
2. Take the end in one hand and cross it over the end in your other hand.
3. Then, take the end you have crossed over on the top and wrap it around the bottom.
4. Now, take both ends of the rope and repeat the same process of wrapping one end around the other.
5. Pull both ends to tighten.

Bowline Knot

The bowline knot creates a fixed loop at the end of your cordage. So, you'll have a line with a circle at the end of it. The loop is not adjustable, so you need to determine the size before tightening the knot. The rope will be secured tightly and will not slip at all. This knot can support a lot of weight, and it is easy to untie even after having carried a heavy load. This knot has been used for rock climbing and in rescue missions. It originated on sailboats and was used to secure the anchors and sails. The bowline knot is your best option for any situation where you need an immovable loop at the end of your cordage.

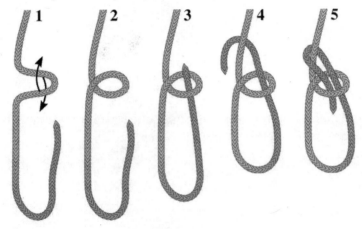

Bowline knot.
Buz11, CC BY-SA 4.0 <https://creativecommons.org/licenses/by-sa/4.0>, via Wikimedia Commons. https://commons.wikimedia.org/wiki/File:Bowline_tying.png

How to Tie a Bowline Knot:

1. Start by creating a loop.
2. Take the working end of your cordage, wrap it around the bottom of the loop, and then thread it through the center of the hole you have created. You should now have two loops – the smaller, original loop and the second, bigger one you have just made.
3. Grab the working end you have threaded through the first smaller loop and wrap it underneath the standing end.
4. Take the working end and thread it back through the original loop.
5. Then, pull on the standing end and working end to tighten the knot.

Bowline on a Bight

This is a variation of the bowline knot that you have just learned. This knot is a little more complicated, but if you follow the instructions carefully, you can master it without much effort. This knot allows you to create a loop in any section of the rope if the end is not available or does not work for what you want to achieve. The loop created by the bowline on a bight has been used for a toe hold in emergencies and also for climbing. Like a traditional bowline, the support knot is strong. It won't slip, but it is easy to untie.

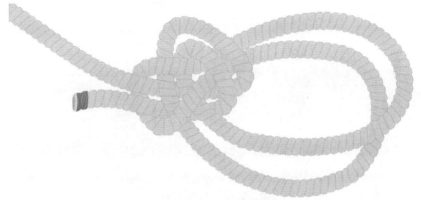

Bowline on a Bight.

SuperManu, CC BY-SA 3.0 <https://creativecommons.org/licenses/by-sa/3.0>, via Wikimedia Commons. https://commons.wikimedia.org/wiki/File:Bowline_on_a_bight-noeud_de_chaise_double_sur_son_double.svg

How to Tie a Bowline on a Bight:

1. Grab a double section of rope to form a loop.
2. Take the working end and push it through the center of the loop.
3. Separate the working end by bringing it to the bottom of your double loop.
4. Thread the double loop through the eye you have created by separating the sections of the working end.
5. Hold the standing end and pull on the double loop to tighten the knot.

Granny Knot

The granny knot is similar to the square knot, so it is usually used to tie bundles together or a rope onto an object. The knot isn't as strong as the square knot, so it is not used as often. Most of the time, you would opt to use the square knot instead of the granny knot, but it helps to have several options. You cannot use a granny knot to secure two ropes because it can easily become undone with a heavy load. This knot is often used for jewelry or for bracelets.

Granny knot.
https://commons.wikimedia.org/wiki/File:Granny_knot.svg

How to Tie a Granny Knot:

1. Start by overlapping two ends of your cordage.
2. Fold over one section of your cordage, pass it over, and then put it through the other end.
3. Pass the opposite end through the loop you have created and pull to tighten.

Figure 8 Knot

The figure 8 is also known as a Flemish knot. Climbers often use this knot as a stopper because it will jam against a cord, which helps to block it. The knot can be easily undone, and it is used so that a climber can quickly untie it as they move swiftly up the mountain to the tippy-top. You should be careful when using this knot as a stopper that takes too much weight because, under great pressure, it can become undone. This knot is a chunky double layer the end of it.

Figure 8 knot.
USCG PTC Developer, CC BY-SA 4.0 <https://creativecommons.org/licenses/by-sa/4.0>, via Wikimedia Commons. https://commons.wikimedia.org/wiki/File:Loop-figure_8-ABoK_1047-USCG.jpg

How to Tie a Figure 8 Knot:

1. Pass your working end over your standing end to form a loop.
2. Lift up and move the working end beneath and around the standing end.
3. Then, pass the working end over and through the original loop you created.
4. Pull to tighten.

Slip Knot

A slip knot is also used as a stopper, much like the figure 8 knot, because it is easy to untie. This knot is also used in knitting and in crochet projects. A slip knot can also be applied for hauling or trapping because it tightens as you pull on it. The knot can also be utilized to secure objects, but it should not take on a heavy load because it might come loose.

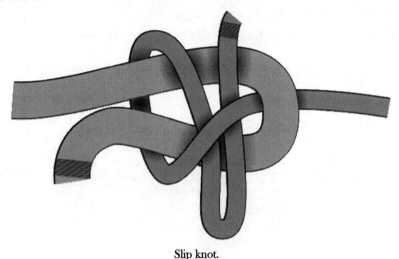

Slip knot.
https://commons.wikimedia.org/wiki/File:Slippendeschootsteek.svg

How to Tie a Slip Knot:

1. Fold your cordage to create an open loop.
2. Grab your working end, create another loop, and then run the end over the two parallel lines you have created with your first open loop.
3. After taking the working end over the two sections of the standing line, wrap it under the line and thread it through the second loop you created.
4. Wrap it around the two sections and through the second loop another two times before pulling on the loop and the working end to tighten it.
5. You should then be able to slide the knot up or down to extend or shrink the loop.

Half Hitch

This knot is used to secure a rope against a solid object, like a pole or a tree. It can tie down valuables you don't want to lose in a wilderness environment. This knot is also great for securing a tent or putting up a clothesline in the yard.

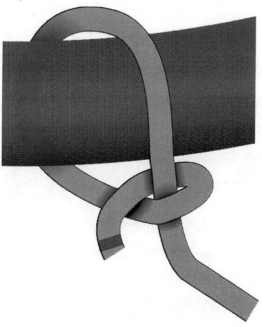

Half hitch.
https://commons.wikimedia.org/wiki/File:Halvesteek.svg

How to Tie a Half Hitch:

1. Start by wrapping your rope around a column to form a bight.
2. Grab your working end and cross it over your standing end to form a loop around the column.
3. Thread the working end through your loop underneath the standing end.
4. Pull to tighten before taking your working end back over your loop and around the column to form another loop.
5. Tuck the working end underneath the standing end and thread it back through the new loop you created.
6. Pull on the working end to tighten.

Two Half Hitches

This knot is a form of the half hitch, and it can be applied in many situations. This strong knot is secure, but it can also be easily untied. You can use this knot to put a swing up in the yard or as a bucket handle. Much like the half hitch, it is excellent for securing objects to a solid column. The knot looks almost like a pretzel.

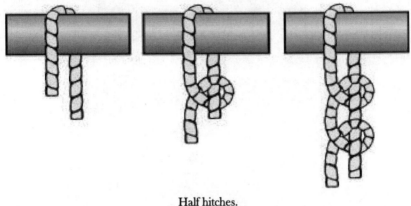

Half hitches.
https://commons.wikimedia.org/wiki/File:Knot_2_half_hitches.jpg.

How to Tie Two-Half Hitches:

1. Create a loop by wrapping your rope around a pole.
2. Next, make a half hitch by passing your working end under your loop.
3. To create another half hitch, wrap the working end around the rope.
4. This variation is slightly more secure than your standard half hitch.

Overhand Knot

The overhand knot is extremely solid to the point that it can sometimes be a disadvantage because it will jam and can be difficult to untie. When using this knot, you should be sure that you want to tie it permanently, or else you will risk having to cut your cordage. This knot can be used to seal up parcels or to secure items that you have no reason to move. You can tie this knot at the end of your cordage to prevent it from fraying. This is one of the first knots many people learn to tie.

Overhand knot.
https://commons.wikimedia.org/wiki/File:Boys%27_Life,_1_-_Overhand_Knots.png.

How to Tie an Overhand Knot:
1. Start by creating a loop.
2. Thread your working end underneath the standing end.
3. Lastly, thread the working end through the loop before pulling it to tighten.

Test Your Skills and Knowledge

1. Which simple knot is used when you tie your shoelaces?
2. Name one use of a bowline knot.
3. Why is it important to know how to tie a variety of knots?
4. Name two knots that can be used as stoppers.
5. Why is using a square knot better than a granny knot?
6. What is another name for a figure 8 knot?
7. What can a slip knot be used for?
8. Choose one of the knot variations you have learned that seems complicated, and try it with some cordage you have nearby.
9. Which knots do climbers make use of?
10. Which knot would you use if you want to tie two ropes of different thicknesses together?

Section 4: Nautical Knots

\Nautical knots are the backbone of sailing, boating, and maritime activities. These knots ensure vessel safety, security, and functionality. From securing lines to preventing accidents and damage, the importance of these knots cannot be overstated. Learning about these knots will make your seagoing adventures fun and practical.

Nautical knots are the backbone of maritime activities.
Marek Slusarczyk, CC BY 3.0 <https://creativecommons.org/licenses/by/3.0>, via Wikimedia Commons. https://commons.wikimedia.org/wiki/File:002_Chrome_steel_boat_cleat_with_tied_mooring_rope_-_nautical_vessel_equipment_detail,_yacht_cleat.jpg

Ensuring Safety

The primary objective of nautical knots is to contribute to the vessel's safety and everyone on board. Well-tied knots prevent lines from coming loose, which is particularly crucial during adverse weather conditions or challenging situations at sea.

Mastery of Basic Nautical Knots

Sailing the seas is way cooler when you know some basic nautical knots. These knots help with everything from tying your boat to the dock to making loops that can do all sorts of handy things. Plus, learning these knots is not just useful but also pretty fun and good for your brain, helping you get better at moving your hands and fingers just right.

Why Nautical Knots Rock:

- They're essential for doing all sorts of important boat stuff like anchoring and managing sails.
- Knowing the right knot for the job makes everything safer and smoother on the water.

Knots and Culture:

- Tying knots is a big deal in sea culture, with some knots being special to certain places or boats.
- Sharing knot skills is a cool way to keep the sea's traditions alive and feel connected to other sailors from the past and present.

Spotlight on the Clove Hitch: This knot is super handy and easy to tie, great for securing stuff on boats or even making a quick handle. It's simple but really strong.

The Clove Hitch knot is super handy and easy to tie.
Cobanyastigi, CC0, via Wikimedia Commons:
https://commons.wikimedia.org/wiki/File:Truckers%27_Hitch_With_Clove_Hitch_Secured_Shee ep_Shank_as_upper_loop.jpg

How to Tie a Clove Hitch:

1. Wrap the rope around something sturdy, like a post.
2. Cross the rope over itself to make an 'X.'
3. Wrap it around again the same way.
4. Slip the end under the last wrap to lock it in place. Make sure the end comes out on the opposite side from where it started.

Learning these knots makes you part of a cool tradition and gives you some serious skills for your next sea adventure!

The Cleat Hitch: A Sailor's BFF

22 is perfect for tying a rope to those T-shaped things on docks and boats (those are called cleats). It's strong, easy to tie, and super important for keeping boats where they should be.

How to Tie It:

1. Start by looping the rope around the bottom part of the cleat, away from where the rope will be pulled.
2. Cross the rope over to the other side of the cleat.
3. Make a figure-eight around the two arms of the cleat for extra hold.
4. Finish by looping the rope around one arm of the cleat to keep it in place.

This knot is all about using friction to keep the rope from moving. The more loops you make, the stronger it will hold. It's easy to untie, too, which is great for when you need to move your boat quickly.

Uses and Tips:

- Super for docking boats.
- Keep the tension even while wrapping to make sure the knot stays strong.

Knowing how to tie a Cleat Hitch makes boat docking and securing ropes a breeze. Just remember to loop, cross, and wrap it tight!

The Cool Sheet Bend Knot

The Sheet Bend is an awesome knot that's great at tying together two ropes, even if they're different sizes or types. It's easy to tie, really strong, and super handy in lots of situations.

How to Tie It:

1. Make a loop (like a little U) in the thicker rope.
2. Take the thinner rope and push it up through the loop.
3. Wrap the thinner rope around the loop and back under itself.
4. Pull the end of the thinner rope tight while holding the rest of the ropes. Now you've got a tight and secure knot!

The Sheet Bend is perfect for when you need to tie ropes together that aren't the same, and it stays strong when there's a lot of pull on it. Plus, it's easy to untie, which is great when you need to change things up quickly.

The Anchor Bend Knot: A Sailor's Best Friend

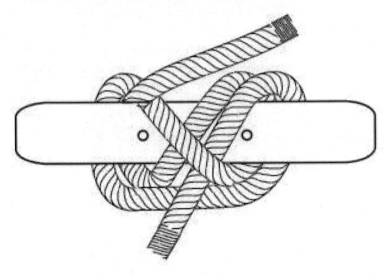

The Anchor Bend knot is super strong – perfect for tying a rope to an anchor or chain. Quatrostein, CC BY-SA 3.0 <https://creativecommons.org/licenses/by-sa/3.0>, via Wikimedia Commons: https://commons.wikimedia.org/wiki/File:Kikkersteek.png

The Anchor Bend knot is super strong – perfect for tying a rope to an anchor or chain. It's good at holding tight and handling sudden tugs, making it a top choice for anchoring boats safely.

How to Tie It:

1. Make a small loop at the end of your rope.
2. Wrap the end around the main part of the rope and the loop a few times.
3. Tuck the end back through the wraps and pull everything tight. Now you've got a super strong connection!

Why It's Awesome:

- It's great at spreading out the pull on the rope, which means less breakage risk.
- Perfect for when the sea gets choppy, and the anchor moves around a lot.

Staying Safe on the Water: Tying your boat or anchor the right way is super important. If not done correctly, it could lead to accidents, like your boat floating away or bumping into things. Here's why getting your knots right matters:

- **Avoiding Oops Moments:** If a boat isn't tied up properly, it could drift off and cause a mess, like bumping into other boats or the dock.
- **Chill Anchoring:** When you drop anchor in a nice spot, using the Anchor Bend keeps your boat from moving too much, so you can relax or swim without worry.
- **Teamwork Makes the Dream Work:** In races, quickly changing your sails using knots like the Sheet Bend can help you adjust to the wind fast and keep you safe.

Learning knots like the Anchor Bend can make your boating safer and more fun, letting you enjoy the water without stress.

Kayaking and Knots: Keeping Paddles Safe

When kayaking, using figure-eight knots on paddle leashes is super smart. These knots act like stoppers, so your paddle doesn't slip away into the river if things get wild. This ensures your important gear stays with you, letting you focus on the adventure without worrying about losing anything important.

Knots in Sea Stories and Teamwork

Sailors have some cool traditions with knots. For example, wearing a Turk's Head knot on your wrist is like having a lucky charm for protection at sea. These traditions show how special and meaningful knots can be in the sailing world.

Working together to learn knots can also help sailors become closer as a team and feel connected to the long history of sea exploration, where knots were key for staying safe.

Learning how to tie knots right is super important. It keeps everyone safe on the water, avoids mishaps, and keeps the spirit of sailing alive. It's not just about tying ropes; it's about being part of a team and respecting the sea's challenges and traditions.

Section 5: Knots for Outdoor Adventures

When engaging in outdoor activities like climbing, camping, or bushcraft, having a solid grasp of essential skills, particularly knot tying, is paramount. This section focuses on fundamental climbing knots, each crucial in ensuring safety and practicality during various outdoor adventures.

Climbing knot.
Mattmaxon at the English-language Wikipedia, CC BY-SA 3.0 <http://creativecommons.org/licenses/by-sa/3.0/>, via Wikimedia Commons. https://commons.wikimedia.org/wiki/File:Stein_knot_AKA_stone_knot.JPG

Climbing Knots for Safe Adventures

Knowing climbing knots is important for having fun and staying safe on hiking and climbing trips. Let's check out some key knots that you'll want to know:

Bachmann Knot

This one's great for moving up ropes or rocks smoothly. It helps you climb without slipping back down. The Bachmann knot is perfect for climbers needing a dependable friction hitch. Used for ascending or descending ropes, it's sturdy, adjustable, and simple to untie.

How to Tie It:

1. Create a loop in the rope, ensuring it's big enough to fit around your harness or attachment point.
2. Pass the loop underneath the main rope and then wrap it around the main rope once more, forming a double wrap.
3. Thread the loop through itself, making sure it passes over the wraps you've created.
4. Pull both ends of the rope to tighten the knot securely onto the main rope.

Tips:

- Ensure you make tight and secure double wraps around the main rope.
- Easily slide the knot up or down the rope as needed by releasing tension.
- To untie, release tension and push the loop through the wraps.
- Practice tying and untying until you're confident in your ability to tie it correctly.

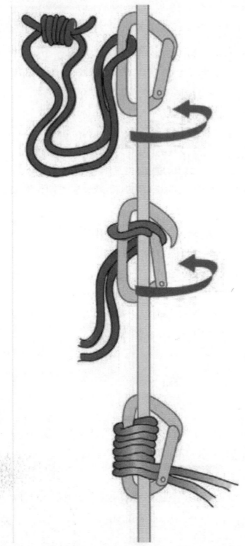

The Bachmann knot is great for moving up ropes or rocks smoothly.
https://commons.wikimedia.org/wiki/File:Bachmann_knot2.png

Klemheist Knot

If you need to climb up a rope or get yourself out of a tricky spot, the Klemheist Knot is your go-to. It's awesome for making sure you can pull yourself up easily. Its gripping capability makes it ideal for ascending or descending ropes, as well as for securing loads or creating makeshift handles.

How to Tie It:

1. Start by forming a small loop in the rope, leaving enough slack for the desired grip size.
2. Pass the loop behind the main rope and then bring it back over itself to form a simple loop.
3. Wrap the loop around the main rope several times, typically 3 to 5 wraps depending on the thickness of the rope and the desired grip strength.
4. Pass the working end of the loop through the initial loop you created.
5. Pull both ends of the rope to cinch the knot tight against the main rope.

The Klemheist knot relies on friction to hold onto the main rope securely. You can easily adjust the position of the knot along the main rope by loosening and sliding it to the desired location. To release the knot, simply push the wraps down the main rope, allowing them to loosen and the knot to untie.

Always perform safety checks to ensure the knot is tied correctly and securely before relying on it for support or load-bearing tasks.

Klemheist Knot.
StromBer 13:33, 21. Mär. 2008 (CET), CC BY-SA 2.0 DE
<https://creativecommons.org/licenses/by-sa/2.0/de/deed.en>, via Wikimedia Commons.
https://commons.wikimedia.org/wiki/File:KlemheistKnot2-4X.jpg

Autoblock Knot

The Autoblock knot, also known as the French Prusik, is a crucial knot in the arsenal of climbers. It's a backup or safety knot, providing friction and security on a climbing rope. This knot comes handy in situations where climbers need to secure themselves while belaying or rappelling.

How to Tie It:

1. Begin by forming a small loop in the rope, leaving enough slack for the desired grip size.
2. Pass the loop behind the main rope and then bring it back over itself to form a simple loop.
3. Wrap the loop around the main rope several times, usually 4 to 6 wraps depending on the thickness of the rope and the desired friction.
4. Pass the working end of the loop through the initial loop you created, creating a girth hitch around the main rope.
5. Pull both ends of the rope to cinch the knot tight against the main rope, ensuring the wraps are snug and secure.
6. To release the knot, simply push the wraps down the main rope, allowing them to loosen and the knot to untie.

Always perform safety checks to ensure the knot is tied correctly and securely before relying on it for support.

The Autoblock knot.
Cobanyastigi, CC0, via Wikimedia Commons:
https://commons.wikimedia.org/wiki/File:AutoblockBagi.JPG

Double Fisherman's Knot

Need to tie two ropes together? The Double Fisherman's Knot is super strong and reliable, perfect for making longer ropes or creating strong anchor points. Its strength and security make it popular in climbing, mountaineering, and other outdoor activities where reliable connections are essential.

How to Tie It:

1. Lay the two ends of the ropes parallel to each other, overlapping by at least a foot.
2. Take one end and wrap it around both ropes, passing it under and then over both ropes. Repeat this wrapping motion three times, ensuring each wrap is snug and parallel to the others.
3. After completing the wraps, thread the working end through the three wraps from the same direction. This creates a loop around both ropes.
4. Now, take the other end of the rope and repeat the wrapping process in the opposite direction. Wrap it around both ropes, passing it under and then over both ropes three times.
5. After completing the wraps, thread this end through the three wraps from the opposite direction. Ensure the knot is tight and secure.
6. Pull both ends of the ropes simultaneously to tighten the knot securely. Ensure the wraps are neat and snug against the ropes.

Learning to tie the double Fisherman's knot is essential for anyone involved in activities that require joining ropes together securely. With its strength and reliability, it's a knot that climbers and outdoor enthusiasts depend on in critical situations.

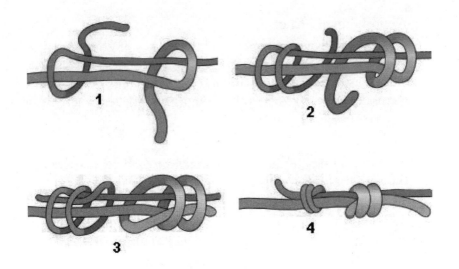

The Double Fisherman's Knot.
https://commons.wikimedia.org/wiki/File:Doppio_inglese_2.png

Figure-Eight Knot

This is a basic but super important knot for tying into your harness or making loops in your rope. It's easy to learn and really secure. It's primarily used to create a secure stopper at the end of a rope, preventing it from sliding through a belay device or anchor point. Its simplicity and reliability make it indispensable for climbers, cavers, sailors, and rescue personnel.

How to Tie It:

1. Begin by forming a small loop in the rope, leaving enough slack for the desired size of the knot.
2. Pass the working end of the rope through the loop from underneath, making sure the rope crosses over itself.
3. Bring the working end around the standing part of the rope, forming a loop that passes behind the standing part.
4. Pass the working end back through the original loop created in step 1, ensuring it follows the same path.
5. Pull both ends of the rope to tighten the knot securely. Ensure the knot is dressed neatly, with no twists or tangles.

FIG. 9   FIG. 10

FIGS. 9 and 10.—Figure-eight knots.

Figure eight knot.
CharlesRKiss, CC BY-SA 4.0 <https://creativecommons.org/licenses/by-sa/4.0>, via Wikimedia Commons. https://commons.wikimedia.org/wiki/File:Figure_Eight_Knot.png

Learning and practicing these knots will make your climbing adventures way safer and more fun. It's all about getting the hang of them so you can use them easily when you're out exploring.

Mastering Rigging Knots

In outdoor activities, the ability to tie effective rigging knots is foundational for tasks such as setting up tents, constructing shelters, or building structures in bushcraft scenarios. Let's delve into a selection of key rigging knots, understanding their applications and mastering the art of secure and reliable tying.

Taut Line Hitch

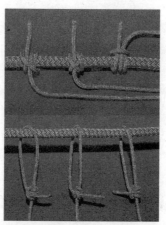

The taut line hitch is prized for its ability to create an adjustable loop that holds tension without slipping.
David J. Fred, CC BY-SA 2.5 <https://creativecommons.org/licenses/by-sa/2.5>, via Wikimedia Commons: https://commons.wikimedia.org/wiki/File:AdjustableHitchVariations.jpg

The taut line hitch is prized for its ability to create an adjustable loop that holds tension without slipping. Employ the taut line hitch when setting up tent guy lines or constructing shelters, allowing for easy adjustment to changing conditions.

How to Tie It:

1. Start by forming a loop in the rope, leaving enough slack for the desired size of the hitch.
2. Pass the working end of the rope around the standing part (the main length of the rope) from behind, creating a loop.
3. Bring the working end around the standing part once more, creating a second loop parallel to the first one.
4. Thread the working end through both loops from underneath, ensuring it follows the same path.
5. Pull the working end to tighten the knot securely. To adjust the tension of the line, simply slide the hitch along the standing part of the rope.

You already know about the clove hitch, which is used to secure a line to a post or a pole. You can also utilize the clove hitch when constructing outdoor structures, tying off ropes to create stable connections.

Timber Hitch

Timber hitch knot.
Attribution-ShareAlike 3.0 Unported, CC BY-SA 3.0 DEED
<*https://creativecommons.org/licenses/by-sa/3.0/deed.en* >
https://commons.wikimedia.org/wiki/File:Timber_Hitch_Final.jpg

The timber hitch excels at gripping round things (think trees), making it efficient for securing loads to poles or branches. Its ability to grip tightly under tension makes it a good choice for hauling and securing loads in various settings, from logging to outdoor construction projects.

How to Tie It:

1. Begin by wrapping the rope around the object you're securing, making at least two full turns.
2. After wrapping the rope, cross the working end over the standing part (the main length of the rope).
3. Bring the working end under the wraps you made around the object.
4. Pull the working end to tighten the knot securely against the object. Ensure the wraps are snug and evenly spaced.

Despite its tight grip, the Timber Hitch is relatively easy to release after bearing a load, making it convenient for temporary applications. For added security, you can tie a Half Hitch after the Timber Hitch to prevent it from slipping.

Prusik Knot

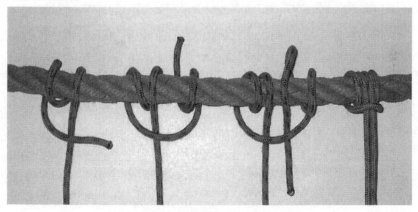

Prusik Knot.
StromBer 19:54, 22. Mär. 2008 (CET), CC BY-SA 2.0 DE
<*https://creativecommons.org/licenses/by-sa/2.0/de/deed.en*>, *via Wikimedia Commons.*
https://commons.wikimedia.org/wiki/File:PrusikNormalgeschlagen.jpg

Named after Austrian mountaineer Karl Prusik, the prusik knot is a versatile hitch that grips a rope when tensioned but slides smoothly when loosened. You can tie the prusik knot to create adjustable attachment points on climbing or rigging ropes during bushcraft activities. It's valued for its ability to grip a rope securely when tensioned, allowing climbers to ascend or descend ropes safely, as well as for various rescue scenarios.

How to Tie It:
1. Begin by forming a small loop in a piece of smaller diameter cord or rope, known as the prusik loop.
2. Pass the prusik loop around the main rope (the rope you'll be ascending or descending), ensuring it crosses over itself.
3. Wrap the prusik loop around the main rope several times, typically 3 to 5 wraps depending on the diameter of the ropes and the desired friction.
4. Pass the end of the Prusik loop through itself, creating a girth hitch around the main rope. Make sure the loop passes over the wraps you've created.
5. Pull both ends of the Prusik loop and the main rope simultaneously to tighten the knot securely.

Trucker's Hitch

Trucker's Hitch.
StromBer, CC0, via Wikimedia Commons.
https://commons.wikimedia.org/wiki/File:TruckHitch_024.jpg

The trucker's hitch is a knot that provides plenty of strong tension for holding loads on the back of the truck. Use this knot when typing down heavy outdoor structures or loads. It provides a mechanical advantage that allows you to tighten the rope securely, making it a great knot for transportation, camping, and various outdoor activities where a strong and reliable tie-down is essential.

How to Tie It:

1. Begin by forming a loop in the rope near the object you're securing. This loop will serve as the anchor point for the knot.
2. Take the working end of the rope and pass it through the loop, creating a slip knot-like configuration.
3. Pull the working end of the rope away from the anchor point and pass it around the object you're securing.
4. Bring the working end of the rope back towards the anchor point and pass it through the loop you created earlier, essentially creating a loop around the standing part of the rope.
5. Pull the working end of the rope to tighten the knot securely. This will create tension on the rope, effectively securing the load.
6. To prevent the knot from loosening, finish off with one or two half hitches around the standing part of the rope.

Mastering Essential Fishing Knots

For anglers, learning the best fishing knots is basic to the sport; those hooks and lures must stay on the line! Let's delve into key fishing knots, understand their applications, and master the art of knot tying for a successful and enjoyable fishing experience.

Palomar Knot

Palomar knot.
Vaughan Pratt, CC BY-SA 3.0 <https://creativecommons.org/licenses/by-sa/3.0>, via Wikimedia Commons, https://commons.wikimedia.org/wiki/File:PalomarKnotSequence.jpg

The Palomar Knot is a popular knot among anglers for its simplicity and strength. It's particularly well-suited for tying fishing line to hooks, swivels, or lures. With its reliable hold and ease of tying, the palomar Knot is a go-to choice for many fishing enthusiasts.

How to Tie It:

1. Double the fishing line and pass it through the eye of the hook, swivel, or lure, creating a loop.
2. Tie a simple overhand knot with the doubled line, leaving a loop large enough to pass the hook, swivel, or lure through.
3. Pass the hook, swivel, or lure through the loop created by the overhand knot.
4. Moisten the knot with water or saliva to reduce friction, then pull both ends of the line to tighten the knot securely against the eye of the hook, swivel, or lure.
5. Trim any excess line extending beyond the knot, leaving a small tag end for added security.
6. Always inspect the palomar Knot after tying to ensure it's tightened securely and there are no signs of slippage or weakness.

Improved Clinch Knot

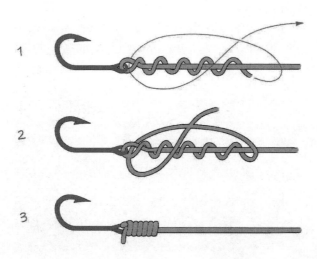

The Improved Clinch Knot

The Improved Clinch Knot is a classic knot used by anglers to tie fishing lines to hooks, lures, or swivels. It's known for its reliability, strength, and ease of tying, making it a favorite among fishermen of all skill levels.

How to Tie It:

1. Pass the end of the fishing line through the eye of the hook or lure, ensuring you leave enough line to work with.
2. Take the tag end (the loose end of the line) and wrap it around the standing line (the main line) at least five or six times. Ensure the wraps are neat and tightly wound.
3. After completing the wraps, thread the tag end through the loop formed between the eye of the hook and the wraps. This creates a new loop near the eye of the hook.
4. Pass the tag end through the loop you just created. This will form a second loop around the standing line.
5. Moisten the knot with water or saliva to reduce friction, then pull both the tag end and the standing line simultaneously to tighten the knot securely against the eye of the hook or lure.
6. Trim any excess tag end extending beyond the knot, leaving a small tag for added security.

Uni-Knot (Duncan Loop)

Uni-knot.
StromBer 11:52, 31. Mär. 2008 (CEST), CC BY-SA 2.0 DE
<https://creativecommons.org/licenses/by-sa/2.0/de/deed.en>, *via Wikimedia Commons:*
https://commons.wikimedia.org/wiki/File:Arborknoten2.JPG

The uni-knot, also known as the Duncan loop, offers strength and versatility, making it suitable for various fishing applications. Use the uni-knot for connecting hooks, swivels, or lures to your fishing line, providing a robust and adaptable knot.

How to Tie It:

1. Pass the end of the fishing line through the eye of the hook or lure, leaving a few inches of tag end to work with.
2. Form a small loop by doubling back the tag end of the line parallel to the standing line (the main line).
3. Take the tag end and wrap it around both the doubled line and the standing line, making at least 4 to 6 wraps. Ensure the wraps are neat and tightly wound.
4. After completing the wraps, pass the tag end back through the loop you created in step 2, entering from the same side as the original tag end.
5. Moisten the knot with water or saliva to reduce friction, then pull both the tag end and the standing line simultaneously to tighten the knot securely against the eye of the hook or lure.
6. Trim any excess tag end extending beyond the knot, leaving a small tag for added security.

Surgeon's Knot

Surgeon's knot.
Attribution-ShareAlike 3.0 Unported, CC BY-SA 3.0 DEED
<*https://creativecommons.org/licenses/by-sa/3.0/deed.en* >
https://commons.wikimedia.org/wiki/File:Surgeon%27s_knot.jpg

The surgeon's knot excels at joining two lines together. Anglers often use it to tie leader material to fishing line or to attach two pieces of fishing line together. Use it when attaching leaders, adding to your fishing line, or creating strong connections between lines of different diameters.

How to Tie It:

1. Lay the ends of the two lines parallel to each other, overlapping by a few inches.
2. Tie a simple overhand knot by passing one end of the line over the other and then threading it back through the loop created.
3. Pass the same end of the line through the loop again, creating a double overhand knot. Do not tighten it completely yet.
4. Repeat steps 2 and 3 with the end of the other line, tying another double overhand knot around the standing part of the first line.
5. Moisten the knots with saliva or water to lubricate them, then pull both ends of the lines simultaneously to tighten the knots securely together. Ensure both knots snug up against each other.
6. Trim any excess tag ends close to the knots, leaving a small tag for added security.

Blood Knot

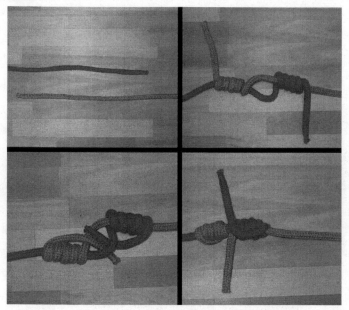

Blood knot.
Chris 73 / Wikimedia Commons CC BY-SA 3.0 DEED
<https://creativecommons.org/licenses/by-sa/3.0/deed.en>
https://commons.wikimedia.org/wiki/File:BloodKnot_HowTo.jpg

The blood knot is ideal for seamlessly joining two lines of similar diameter, maintaining strength and integrity. Use the blood knot when creating leaders or connecting sections of fishing lines.

How to Tie It:

1. Lay the ends of the two lines parallel to each other, overlapping by several inches.
2. Tie a simple overhand knot by passing one end of the line over the other and then threading it back through the loop created. Do not tighten it completely yet.
3. Starting with one end, wrap it around the standing part of the other line, making at least five wraps. Ensure the wraps are neat and tightly wound.
4. Repeat step 3 with the other end of the line, wrapping it around the standing part of the first line in the opposite direction.
5. After completing the wraps with both ends, pass each end through the middle of the wraps, entering from opposite directions.
6. Moisten the knots with saliva or water to lubricate them, then pull both ends of the lines simultaneously to tighten the knots securely together. Ensure both knots snug up against each other.
7. Trim any excess tag ends close to the knots, leaving a small tag for added security.

Arbor Knot

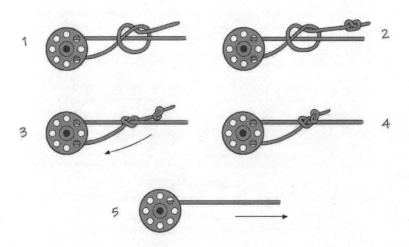

Arbor knot

The arbor knot is designed for securing a fishing line to the reel, ensuring a reliable connection between your line and the spool. Use this knot when spooling a new line onto your fishing reel; you'll have a secure attachment and get great performance from your reel.

How to Tie:
1. Pass the line through the arbor.
2. Tie a simple overhand knot around the line.
3. Wrap the free end around the arbor and standing line.
4. Pass the free end through the overhand knot.
5. Moisten and tighten the knot.
6. Trim excess line.

Loop Knot (Non-Slip Loop Knot)

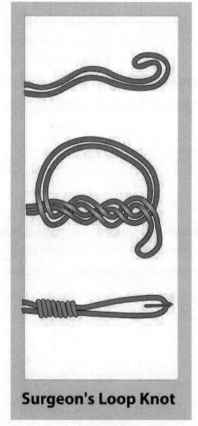

Loop Knot.
https://commons.wikimedia.org/wiki/File:Surgeon%27s_Loop_knot.svg

The loop knot (or non-slip loop knot) enhances lure action by allowing them to move more freely, making it suitable for certain types of lures. Use the loop knot when attaching lures that are designed for increased movement and action in the water.

How to Tie:
1. Form a small loop at the end of the line.
2. Pass the tag end through the loop, then wrap it around the standing line.
3. Pass the tag end back through the loop.
4. Moisten and tighten the knot.

Building Outdoor Structures

Knowing how to build things is super cool when you're on an adventure outside! Learning special knots and ways to tie ropes together is like unlocking a secret power to make strong, awesome stuff outdoors. Here are some key knots that are great for building:

Japanese Square Lashing: This knot is super strong and perfect for making parts of your outdoor fort or anything else stick together really well.

How to Tie:
1. Position two poles at a right angle.
2. Wrap the rope around both poles near the intersection.
3. Make a clove hitch around the vertical pole.
4. Wrap the rope tightly around both poles, making 5-7 wraps.
5. Tie two half hitches around the vertical pole.
6. Tuck the tail under a wrap to finish.
7. Trim excess rope if needed.

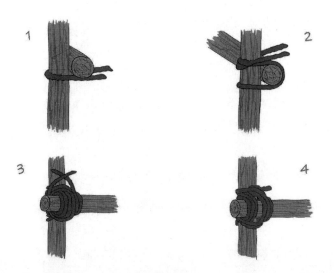

Japanese Square Lashing.

Shear Lashing: This knot keeps things standing if you're building something that might get pushed from the sides.

How To Tie:
1. Position two poles parallel to each other.
2. Place the rope over both poles, leaving a tail hanging.
3. Wrap the rope tightly around both poles, making multiple wraps.
4. Cross the rope between the poles.
5. Wrap the rope around both poles again, going in the opposite direction.
6. Tie two half hitches around one of the poles.
7. Tuck the tail under a wrap to finish.
8. Trim excess rope if needed.

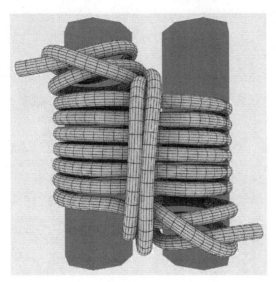
Shear Lashing.
Zaripov Rustem, CC BY-SA 4.0 <https://creativecommons.org/licenses/by-sa/4.0>, via Wikimedia Commons: https://commons.wikimedia.org/wiki/File:Shear_lashing_0_Thumb.jpg

Taut-Line Hitch: This adjustable knot is awesome for making tent lines tighter or looser without a fuss.

How to Tie:

1. Wrap the rope around a fixed object, forming a loop.
2. Pass the free end of the rope through the loop.
3. Wrap the free end around the standing part of the rope.
4. Pass the free end through the loop again, forming a second loop.
5. Tighten the knot by pulling the free end while holding the standing part.
6. Adjust the tension by sliding the knot along the standing part.

Alpine Butterfly Knot: Need a loop in the middle of your rope? This knot's got you covered. It's great for hanging things up or tying stuff down.

1. Form a loop in the rope, crossing one end over the standing part.
2. Bring the end back underneath the standing part, forming a second loop.
3. Cross the end over the first loop and tuck it under the second loop.
4. Pull the ends to tighten the knot, forming the Alpine Butterfly.

Alpine butterfly knot.
Mark A. Taff. http://www.MarkTaff.com, CC BY-SA 3.0 US
<https://creativecommons.org/licenses/by-sa/3.0/us/deed.en>, via Wikimedia Commons:
https://commons.wikimedia.org/wiki/File:Alpine_butterfly_loop.jpg

Practicing these knots means you can make all sorts of cool constructions that hold up when you're exploring the great outdoors. Imagine the amazing camps and shelters you can build!

Survival Knots for the Wild

Being quick and smart with knots can save the day in the wild. Here are some super important knots for survival:

Tourniquet Knot: If someone's hurt and bleeding a lot, this knot can help stop the bleeding until you get help.

1. Wrap a piece of fabric or bandage tightly around the limb above the wound.
2. Tie a half knot with the ends of the fabric, making sure it's snug against the limb.
3. Tie a second half knot on top of the first one, securing the tourniquet in place.
4. Twist a stick or rod into the knot to tighten further if necessary.

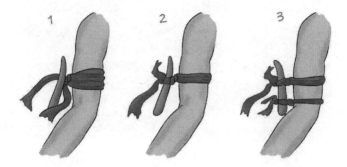

A Tourniquet Knot.

Tripod Lashing: With three sticks and this knot, you can make a sturdy stand for shelters or to hang things up high.

1. Lay three poles parallel to each other, forming a tripod.
2. Tie a clove hitch around one of the poles near the top.
3. Wrap the rope tightly around all three poles, making multiple wraps.
4. Finish with two half hitches around one of the poles.
5. Tuck the tail under a wrap to secure.
6. Adjust the tension and position of the lashing as needed.

Fireman's Chair Knot: Need to lift or lower someone in an emergency? This knot makes it possible.

1. Tie a Figure-8 Knot on a bight in the rope to create a loop.
2. Pass the loop around the person's waist to form a harness.
3. Optionally, create leg loops for stability.
4. Tie a second Figure-8 Knot on a bight as a backup.
5. Attach the rope to the harness using a carabiner or secure knot.
6. Lower the person using a belay device or friction knot.
7. Maintain clear communication throughout the process.
8. Perform safety checks on all equipment and knots before lowering.

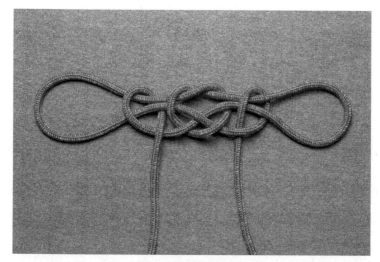

Fireman's Chair Knot.
David J. Fred, CC BY-SA 2.5 <https://creativecommons.org/licenses/by-sa/2.5>, via Wikimedia Commons: https://commons.wikimedia.org/wiki/File:Handcuff-knot-ABOK-1140-Hitch-finish.jpg

Clove Hitch: Fast and easy, this knot lets you tie a rope to a pole or tree super quick, perfect for making shelters or other handy survival tools.

1. Pass the end of the rope around the object you're tying to.
2. Cross the end over the standing part of the rope to form an X.
3. Cross the end under the standing part of the rope, creating a loop.
4. Pass the end over the object and through the loop.
5. Tighten the knot by pulling both ends of the rope.

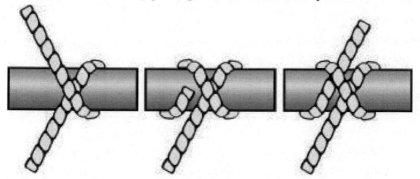

Clove Hitch.
Jazzmanian at English Wikibooks, Public domain, via Wikimedia Commons. https://commons.wikimedia.org/wiki/File:Knot_clove.jpg

Knowing these knots gives you the skills to handle tough spots in nature. Keep practicing, and you'll be ready for anything the wild throws at you.

Section 6: Everyday Knots

Knot tying is a super cool skill that you can use in lots of ways every day! It's perfect for ensuring your tent stays put, building shelters, and keeping your gear safe when camping, hiking, or sailing.

At home, you can use simple knots for things like tying up packages, keeping your shoes on your feet, or keeping your toys and stuff neat and tidy. Knots are also important for people who sail boats, go fishing, or build things because they help make everything safe and work better.

In emergencies, like when someone needs to be rescued, knowing the right knots can be super important. Learning to tie knots can make you better at solving problems, help you do things on your own, and give you handy skills for all kinds of situations.

Single Shoelace Knot

The single shoelace knot, often called the "bunny ears" method, is simple to do! You probably already know this one: start by crossing one shoelace over the other, creating a simple X shape. Then, take one end and pass it under the other lace, pulling it through the loop created. Tighten the knot by pulling both ends at the same time.

Practical Applications

The single shoelace knot is a quick and efficient way to secure footwear. You'll use this every time you put on your sneakers and in many other places around home and school. Look around – you'll see it everywhere!

Double Shoelace Knot

Building on the single knot, the double shoelace knot adds an extra layer of security. After creating the initial knot, repeat the process by crossing one lace over the other and pulling it through the loop again. This creates a double loop, so your knot is extra strong!

Practical Applications

The double shoelace knot is particularly useful in situations where shoes may undergo a lot of action, like sports or P.E. This knot doesn't come loose easily, so you won't have to worry about tripping all over the place!

Everyday Tasks

Knot tying extends beyond shoelaces and finds application in various everyday tasks. For instance, securing bags of snacks with a knot helps preserve freshness, while bundling items together using a knot helps when you're trying to store things.

School and Work

Knots come in handy for securing backpacks or luggage and organizing materials. Students use knots to fasten art supplies, and professionals might use them to bundle cables or secure items during transit.

Recreational Activities

Knot tying is essential during recreational activities such as camping, hiking, and fishing. Whether setting up a tent, securing gear, or even improvising solutions on the spot, the ability to tie different knots becomes very important in the outdoors!

Universal Tools in Daily Life

Single and double shoelace knots are used a lot in our daily lives. Look around: you'll find these knots keeping shoes on tightly and helping keep things organized neatly.

Fisherman's Loop

The Fisherman's Loop, also called the Angler's Loop, is a handy fishing knot.
Malta, CC BY-SA 2.5 <https://creativecommons.org/licenses/by-sa/2.5>, via Wikimedia Commons: https://commons.wikimedia.org/wiki/File:N%C5%93ud_de_p%C3%AAcheur_double_non_serr%C3%A9.jpg

The Fisherman's Loop, also called the *Angler's Loop*, is a handy fishing knot. It makes a strong loop at the end of your line so you can quickly hook on your bait or other gear. Fishermen love it because it never lets them down.

How to Tie the Fisherman's Loop:

1. Start with a basic loop knot in your line.
2. Thread the loose end (that's the tag end) through the loop two times.
3. Wet the knot a bit to make tightening easier.
4. Pull on both the main line and the tag end together to snug it up tight.

Why It's Awesome:

It's perfect for tying on all your fishing stuff securely. It works great for different kinds of fishing, whether in a lake or the ocean.

Not Just for Fishing:

- Use it to make a quick handle on bags or tie things down tightly.
- Great for camping or outdoor stuff when you need a loop that you can trust.

Super Strong Knot:

The Fisherman's Loop keeps most of the line's strength, even under lots of pressure. That means your loop stays tight, even when you've got a big fish on the line!

Bow Tie Knot

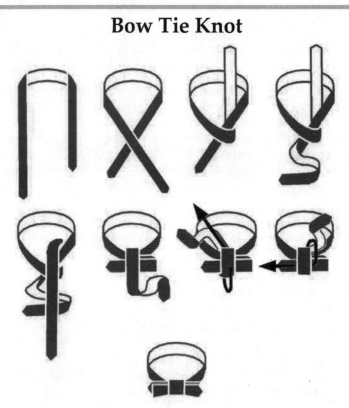

The bow tie knot is a classic and elegant method of tying a necktie.
HowToTieBowtie_VersionA.png: Chris 73derivative work: M.moriconi, CC BY-SA 3.0 <https://creativecommons.org/licenses/by-sa/3.0>, via Wikimedia Commons: https://commons.wikimedia.org/wiki/File:HowToTieBowtie_second-way-A.png

The bow tie knot (also known as the butterfly knot) is a classic and elegant method of tying a necktie. This knot resembles the shape of a bow tie; hence, its name. It is commonly used in formal and semi-formal settings, adding a touch of sophistication to one's attire.

Tying the Bow Tie Knot

1. Begin with the wide end of the tie on your right side and the narrow end on your left.
2. Cross the wide end over the narrow end.
3. Bring the wide end around and behind the narrow end, creating a loop.
4. Pull the wide end up and through the loop.
5. Tighten the knot by adjusting the ends and the bow's size.

Practical Applications

The bow tie knot is primarily used with neckties, especially when aiming for a refined and stylish appearance. It is often chosen for formal events, weddings, or any occasion with a desired touch of elegance.

Alternatives to the Bow Tie Knot

While the bow tie knot is a classic choice for formal occasions, various alternative knots offer versatility and cater to different collar types, tie widths, and personal styles. Experimenting with different knots allows individuals to express their fashion preferences and adapt their necktie choices to various settings.

Four-in-Hand Knot

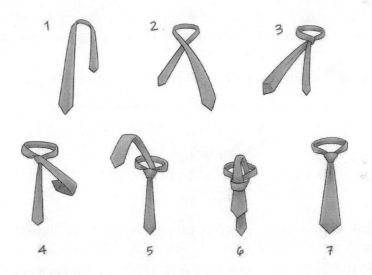

Four-in-Hand Knot.

The Four-in-Hand Knot is one of the most classic and widely used necktie knots. It's known for its simplicity, versatility, and slightly asymmetric appearance. Named after the carriage drivers of the 19th century who tied their scarves with this knot, the Four-in-Hand is suitable for most occasions, from casual to business settings.

How to Tie It:

1. Start by draping the tie around your neck with the wide end on your right side and the narrow end on your left side. Adjust the

length so that the wide end is longer than the narrow end.
2. Cross the wide end of the tie over the narrow end, forming an "X" at the front of your neck.
3. Bring the wide end underneath the narrow end, passing it from right to left.
4. Bring the wide end up through the loop around your neck, passing it from underneath to create a diagonal loop on the right side.
5. Bring the wide end across the front of the knot, passing it from right to left.
6. Bring the wide end up through the loop at the front of the knot, passing it from underneath to create a second diagonal loop on the left side.
7. Hold onto the narrow end with one hand and use the other hand to slide the knot up towards your neck, adjusting the tightness and symmetry as desired.
8. Once the knot is tightened to your liking, adjust the collar and the front of the tie to ensure a neat and stylish appearance.

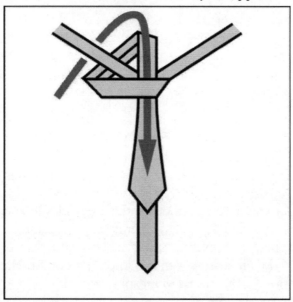

Four-in-Hand knot works great for most ties and looks a bit off-center.
Pumbaa80, bearbeitet von Xubor, CC BY-SA 2.5 <https://creativecommons.org/licenses/by-sa/2.5>, via Wikimedia Commons: https://commons.wikimedia.org/wiki/File:Tie_diagram_l-c-end-better.png

Windsor Knot

Big and shaped like a triangle, this knot fits shirts with wide collars and is awesome for thick ties.

How to Tie It:

1. Start by draping the tie around your neck with the wide end on your right side and the narrow end on your left side. Adjust the length so that the wide end is longer than the narrow end.
2. Cross the wide end of the tie over the narrow end, forming an X at the front of your neck.
3. Bring the wide end underneath the narrow end, passing it from right to left.
4. Now bring the wide end up through the loop around your neck, passing it from underneath to create a diagonal loop on the right side.
5. Bring the wide end across the front of the knot, passing it from left to right.
6. Bring the wide end up through the loop at the front of the knot, passing it from underneath to create a second diagonal loop on the left side.
7. Pass the wide end down through the loop at the front of the knot, creating a third diagonal loop on the right side.
8. Bring the wide end across the front of the knot once more, passing it from right to left.
9. Pass the wide end up through the loop at the front of the knot, creating a fourth diagonal loop on the left side.
10. Hold onto the narrow end with one hand and use the other hand to slide the knot up towards your neck, adjusting the tightness and symmetry as desired.
11. Once the knot is tightened to your liking, adjust the collar and the front of the tie to ensure a neat and symmetrical appearance.

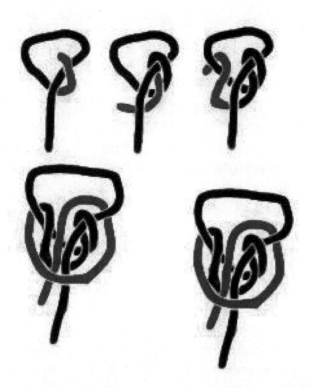

Windsor knot fits shirts with wide collars and is awesome for thick ties.
Fúlvio, CC BY-SA 3.0 <https://creativecommons.org/licenses/by-sa/3.0>, via Wikimedia Commons: https://commons.wikimedia.org/wiki/File:Double_windsor.svg

Half-Windsor Knot

It's not as big as the Windsor, but it's still great for all kinds of events. It goes well with medium-size ties.

How to Tie It:

1. Start by draping the tie around your neck with the wide end on your right side and the narrow end on your left side.
2. Cross the wide end of the tie over the narrow end, forming an X.
3. Bring the wide end underneath the narrow end, passing it from right to left and then across the front of the knot, passing it from left to right.
4. Bring the wide end up through the loop around your neck, passing it from underneath to create a diagonal loop on the right side.
5. Bring the wide end across the front of the knot once more, passing it from right to left.

6. Bring the wide end up through the loop at the front of the knot, passing it from underneath to create a second diagonal loop on the left side.
7. Pass the wide end down through the loop at the front of the knot, creating a third diagonal loop on the right side.
8. Hold onto the narrow end with one hand and use the other hand to slide the knot up towards your neck.
9. Adjust the collar and the front of the tie to ensure a neat appearance.

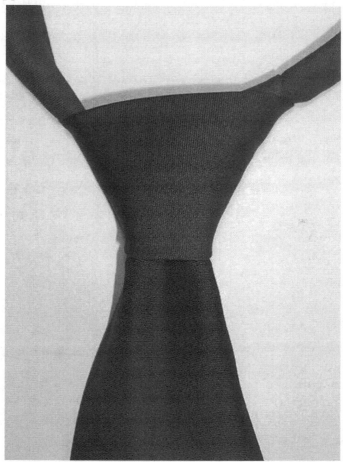

Half-Windsor knot.
No machine-readable author provided. Pumbaa80 assumed (based on copyright claims)., CC BY-SA 2.5 <https://creativecommons.org/licenses/by-sa/2.5>, via Wikimedia Commons. https://commons.wikimedia.org/wiki/File:Necktie_Half-Windsor_knot.jpg

Pratt (Shelby) Knot

Kind of like the Four-in-Hand but tidier and a bit bigger. It's good for just about any tie.

How to Tie It:

1. Start by draping the tie around your neck similar to the above mentioned styles and cross it to form an X.
2. Bring the wide end underneath the narrow end, passing it from right to left.
3. Now bring the wide end up through the loop around your neck, passing it from underneath to create a diagonal loop on the left side.
4. Bring the wide end across the front of the knot, passing it from left to right and up through the loop at the front of the knot, passing it from underneath to create a second diagonal loop on the right side.
5. Create a third diagonal loop on the left side.
6. Adjust the tightness and symmetry as desired.

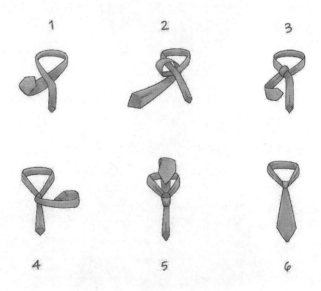

This knot is good for just about any tie.

Eldredge Knot

Named after its creator, Jeffrey Eldredge, this knot is not for the faint of heart but is sure to make a bold statement when worn. While it may take some practice to master, the Eldredge Knot offers a unique and stylish option for those looking to stand out with their neckwear.

How to Tie It:
1. Start by draping like you did in the previous knots.
2. Make an X by crossing the wide end of the tie over the narrow end.
3. Bring the wide end up through the loop around your neck, passing it from underneath to create a diagonal loop on the left side.
4. Bring the wide end across the front of the knot, passing it from left to right.
5. Bring the wide end up through the loop at the front of the knot, passing it from underneath to create a second diagonal loop on the right side.
6. Pass the wide end down through the lower diagonal loop on the right side of the knot.
7. Pass the wide end up through the upper diagonal loop on the right side of the knot.
8. Bring the wide end across the front of the knot once more, passing it from right to left.
9. Pass the wide end down through the loop at the front of the knot, creating a third diagonal loop on the left side.
10. Once the knot is tightened, adjust for a neat look.

Eldredge knot.
Coastal Elite from Halifax, Canada, CC BY-SA 2.0 <https://creativecommons.org/licenses/by-sa/2.0>, via Wikimedia Commons.
https://commons.wikimedia.org/wiki/File:Eldredge_Knot_(23364860284).jpg

Trinity Knot

The Trinity Knot, also known as the Triquetra Knot, is a stylish and intricate necktie knot that resembles a three-pointed Celtic symbol. It's a less common knot choice but offers a unique and eye-catching appearance that is sure to draw attention.

How to Tie It:

1. Drape the tie around your neck and cross it, forming an X at the front of your neck.
2. Bring the wide end up through the loop around your neck, passing it from underneath to create a diagonal loop on the left side.
3. Bring the wide end across the front of the knot, passing it from left to right.
4. Bring the wide end up through the loop at the front of the knot, passing it from underneath to create a second diagonal loop on the right side.
5. Pass the wide end down through the lower diagonal loop on the right side of the knot.
6. Pass the wide end up through the upper diagonal loop on the right side of the knot.

Kelvin Knot

The Kelvin Knot is a lesser-known necktie knot that offers a unique and asymmetrical appearance. Named after the physicist Lord Kelvin, this knot features a distinctive diagonal knot structure that adds an interesting flair to your neckwear. While not as common as some other knots, the Kelvin Knot is a stylish option for those looking to stand out with their tie choice. Here's how to tie it:

How to Tie It:

1. Drape the tie and form an X by crossing the two ends like you did earlier.
2. Bring the wide end underneath the narrow end, passing it to the left side.
3. Bring the wide end up through the loop around your neck, creating a diagonal loop on the left side of the knot.
4. Bring the wide end across the front of the knot, passing it from left to right.
5. Pass the wide end down through the loop at the front of the knot, forming a second diagonal loop on the right side.
6. Adjust for a neat look.

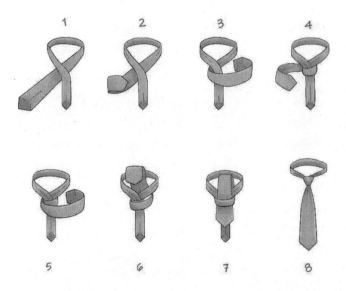

A smaller, easy knot that's perfect for everyday wear and goes well with thin collars and lighter ties.

Oriental Knot

The oriental knot, also known as the simple knot or kent knot, is a classic and elegant necktie knot that is simple to tie and well-suited for thin or wide ties. It has a symmetrical and streamlined appearance, making it a popular choice for both formal and casual occasions.

How to Tie It:

1. Drape the tie around your neck and form a cross.
2. Bring the wide end underneath the narrow end, wrapping it around the narrow end from right to left.
3. Bring the wide end up through the loop around your neck, creating a simple knot.
4. Pass the wide end down through the loop at the front of the knot, tightening it slightly.

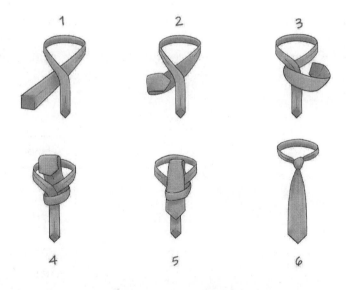

A super simple, tiny knot that's quick to tie

The Cool Parcel Bend Knot

The Parcel Bend Knot.
Cobanyastigi, CC0, via Wikimedia Commons:
https://commons.wikimedia.org/wiki/File:KolanBagi%C3%96n.jpg

The Parcel Bend Knot, also known as the Harness Bend, is a super-strong knot that's perfect for tying together two ropes, even if they're different sizes. It makes sure they stay tightly connected, which is awesome for when you need a really secure tie.

How to Tie It:
1. Place the big rope next to the smaller one so they overlap a bit.
2. Wrap the skinny rope around both ropes a few times.
3. Tuck the end of the skinny rope under and pull it through the loop you made.
4. Pull on both ends of the skinny rope to tighten the knot.

Where to Use It:
- Camping adventures
- Sailing the seas
- Building cool stuff

- Anytime you need to tie ropes together tightly

This knot is great because it won't slip, even if you pull really hard, making it perfect for all kinds of fun activities and important tasks. Whether you're making something or need a quick fix, the Parcel Bend Knot has got your back!

Section 7: Knotting for Fun

Tying knots can help you relax and feel less stressed. It's like doing a calming activity that lets your mind focus on one thing; repetitive and rhythmic; this is like a simple and slow dance for your hands. Doing this can make your mind forget about worries and be present in the moment. It's like a break from the business of the day. Feeling the texture of the rope in your hands is nice, and it's like a little fun challenge to create different knots. Tying knots is not just about making things; it's about taking a quiet moment for yourself, feeling good when you finish, and letting your mind relax. It's like a simple, hands-on way to feel calm and accomplished.

Decorative Knots

Crafting and jewelry-making offer wonderful opportunities to showcase visually appealing, decorative knots. Here are some knots that can add flair to your creations:

Celtic Knot

Celtic knot.
https://commons.wikimedia.org/wiki/File:Celtic-knot-linear-7crossings.svg

The Celtic knot is a symbol of eternity, and its intricate design is visually captivating. This knot involves weaving a continuous cord into a mesmerizing pattern. It's often used in jewelry, especially as pendants or focal points in bracelets.

Instructions:
1. Hold one end of the string in each hand.
2. Cross the right end of the string over the left to make a loop on the left side.
3. Wrap the right end behind the left end and pull it through the loop.
4. Pull both ends to slightly tighten the knot.
5. Repeat steps two to four using the left end of the string.
6. Pull both ends to tighten the knot.

Monkey's Fist

Monkey's fist knot.
No machine-readable author provided. Tortillovsky assumed (based on copyright claims)., CC BY-SA 3.0 <http://creativecommons.org/licenses/by-sa/3.0/>, via Wikimedia Commons: https://commons.wikimedia.org/wiki/File:Knot_Monkey_Fist.jpg

Instructions:

1. Hold the end of the string in your hand and wrap it around your fingers to create a loop.
2. Gently slide the loop off your fingers and hold it between your thumb and index finger.
3. Wrap the string around the loop. Make sure to go in the opposite direction than the one you used to make the first loop. Do this until you have three layers of wraps.
4. Pull the end of the string through the center of the wraps until the knot is tight.

The Monkey's Fist knot is a round, ball-like knot that adds a nautical and decorative touch. It's often used in keychains or as a focal point in necklaces. Vary the size and experiment with different materials for diverse looks.

Chinese Button Knot

The Chinese Button knot is an ornamental knot that resembles a flower. It works well as a decorative closure for bracelets or necklaces, adding a touch of elegance. Play with different thread or cord colors to create a vibrant bloom.

Instructions:

1. Fold the string in half, find its middle point and hold it with one hand.
2. Make a loop with one end of the string and cross it over the other end.
3. Bring the bottom end up through the loop to create a new loop.
4. Pass the end through the new loop, making sure it goes under the first loop.
5. Pull the end through to tighten the knot, forming a button-like shape.

Lover's Knot (Josephine Knot)

Lover's knot.
Frank van Mierlo, Attribution, via Wikimedia Commons:
https://commons.wikimedia.org/wiki/File:True_Lover%27s_knot-0.jpg

Instructions:

1. Hold both ends of the string and tie a simple knot, leaving a loop at the top.
2. Take the left end of the string and make a loop toward the right.
3. Take the right end of the string and make a loop toward the left, then pass the right loop under the left loop.

4. Pass the right string over the left loop and through the right loop, it should look like a pretzel.
5. Pull both ends of the string to tighten the knot.

The Lover's knot is a delicate and romantic knot that creates an intertwined pattern. It's popular in wedding-themed jewelry or as a focal point in elegant accessories like headbands or earrings.

Snake Knot

The Snake knot, resembling the body of a snake, is both visually interesting and versatile. Use it to create bracelets or anklets with a unique and textured design. Experiment with multiple colors for a striking effect.

Instructions:

1. Fold the string in half to find the middle point, make sure to hold this point with one hand.
2. With your other hand, make a loop with one end of the string and cross it over to the other end of your string.
3. Pull the bottom end through a loop to create a new loop and pull the end through to tighten the knot.
4. Repeat steps two to four until you reach the desired length.

Double Coin Knot

Double coin knot.
ClemRutter, CC BY-SA 4.0 <https://creativecommons.org/licenses/by-sa/4.0>, via Wikimedia Commons: https://commons.wikimedia.org/wiki/File:Double_coin_knot_3806.jpg

The Double Coin knot is a round, flat knot that adds a decorative element to accessories. It's ideal for making earrings, pendants, or even embellishments for bags. Vary the size and color to suit your design.

Instructions:

1. Make a loop to the right, then pass one of the end over it without passing it through.
2. Make another loop on the side opposite to the first one.
3. Pass the end under the loops, then over, and then under again. Pull both ends to tighten your knot.

Infinity Knot

Symbolizing eternity, the Infinity knot is a simple yet elegant choice. Incorporate it into necklaces or bracelets to add a touch of symbolism to your jewelry designs.

Diamond Knot (Lanyard Knot)

Lanyard knot.
David J. Fred, CC BY-SA 2.5 <https://creativecommons.org/licenses/by-sa/2.5>, via Wikimedia Commons: https://commons.wikimedia.org/wiki/File:Knife-lanyard-knot-ABOK-787-Final.jpg

The Diamond knot, often used in lanyards, has a distinctive diamond shape. It can either be incorporated into keychains or used as a decorative element in various crafts.

Instructions:
1. Loop a piece of your rope other the three middle fingers on your left hand. Make sure to lay the ends across your palms.
2. Make a loop with the cord on the right.
3. Flip the knot.
4. Loop the bottom cord behind the tail of the top cord.
5. Loop it over the top cord, under the middle, and over the bottom.
6. Center the knot on your palm. It should look similar to a Celtic knot.
7. Pull the top cord towards your thumb and pull it underneath the knot, leaving a little bit of space. Repeat this step with the bottom cord.
8. Pull each of the cords slowly until the knot is tight.

Experimenting with these decorative knots opens up a world of creative possibilities in crafting and jewelry making. Combine different knots and varying materials, and play with colors to express your unique style and create visually stunning pieces.

Creating Friendship Bracelets

Creating friendship bracelets is a fun and creative way to express your personal style. Ra'ike (see also: de:Benutzer:Ra'ike), CC BY-SA 3.0 <http://creativecommons.org/licenses/by-sa/3.0/>, via Wikimedia Commons: https://commons.wikimedia.org/wiki/File:Friendship_Bracelet_square_forms.jpg

Creating friendship bracelets is a fun and creative way to express your personal style and share handmade gifts with friends. Below are step-by-step instructions for a simple diagonal stripe pattern using knotting techniques. Feel free to experiment with color choices to make your bracelet unique.

Materials Needed

- Embroidery floss (choose multiple colors)
- Scissors
- Tape or a safety pin (to secure the bracelet)

Step 1: Gather Materials

Gather your embroidery floss in the desired colors. You can choose as many colors as you like, but for simplicity, let's start with three different colors.

Step 2: Cut the Floss

Cut each color into strands, each about 24 inches long. You'll need two strands of each color. Adjust the length based on your wrist size and the desired length of the bracelet, leaving a little extra for tying knots.

Step 3: Arrange the Colors

Line up the strands side by side, making sure the colors are in the order you want for your bracelet.

Step 4: Secure with Tape or a Safety Pin

Secure one end of the strands with tape or a safety pin. This will make the braiding process easier.

Step 5: Begin Knotting

Start by taking the leftmost strand and making a "4" shape over the next strand (middle strand).

Step 6: Make a Knot

Wrap the leftmost strand behind the middle strand, pulling the end through the loop created by the "4." Pull tight to create a knot.

Step 7: Repeat with the Right Strand

Repeat the process with the rightmost strand. Make a backward "4" over the middle strand, wrap it behind, and pull through the loop.

Step 8: Continue Braiding

Continue alternating between left and right, creating a series of knots. As you progress, you'll see diagonal stripes forming.

Step 9: Add More Colors

If you want to add more colors, simply introduce new strands and continue the knotting pattern.

Step 10: Secure the End

Once your bracelet reaches the desired length, secure the end with a knot. Trim any excess floss.

Step 11: Tie the Bracelet

Tie the bracelet around your wrist, making a double knot to secure it. Trim any remaining excess floss.

Experiment with Patterns

Feel free to experiment with different patterns, such as chevrons, diamonds, or even letters. You can also add beads for extra flair. The key is to have fun and let your creativity shine through in your friendship bracelet designs.

Customize Your Gear

Creating keychains, lanyards, and zipper pulls by using knots is a fantastic and engaging craft activity for children. Not only does it foster creativity, but it also allows kids to personalize and showcase their unique style. Below are step-by-step instructions for making these items by using simple knotting techniques.

Materials Needed

- Assorted colors of paracord or lanyard cord
- Scissors
- Keyrings or clasps (for keychains)
- Swivel clasps (for lanyards)
- Small zipper pulls or clips (for zipper pulls)

Keychain

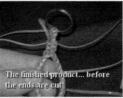

Start by choosing your favorite colors of paracord.

Tuningpeg571, CC BY-SA 3.0 <https://creativecommons.org/licenses/by-sa/3.0>, via Wikimedia Commons: https://commons.wikimedia.org/wiki/File:Lanyard.png

Step 1: Select Colors

Choose your favorite colors of paracord. Cut a length of cord, about 4 feet long, for a standard-sized keychain.

Step 2: Create a Cow Hitch Knot

Fold the cord in half, creating a loop. Pass the folded end through the key ring, then pull the loose ends through the loop, securing the cord to the ring.

Step 3: Begin Braiding

Separate the cords into two sets, each with two strands. Start braiding by using a simple, three-strand braid until you reach the desired length.

Step 4: Tie off the End

Once the braid is long enough, tie off the end with a knot. Trim any excess cord, leaving a small tail.

Step 5: Finishing Touch

Attach a key ring or lobster clasp to the looped end, and your personalized keychain is ready!

Lanyard

Start by selecting your favorite lanyard cord colors.
Auckland Museum, CC BY 4.0 <https://creativecommons.org/licenses/by/4.0>, via Wikimedia Commons: https://commons.wikimedia.org/wiki/File:Lanyard_(AM_1957.67.16-4).jpg

Step 1: Choose Colors

Select your favorite lanyard cord colors. Cut two pieces of cord, each about 5 feet long for a standard lanyard.

Step 2: Secure the Cords

Tie the two cords together at one end, creating a loop. This will be the top of your lanyard.

Step 3: Start a Box Stitch

Separate the cords into two pairs. Cross the left pair over the right pair, creating an "X." Pass the left pair behind the right pair.

Step 4: Continue the Box Stitch

Repeat the box stitch pattern, alternating left and right, until you reach the desired length.

Step 5: Finish and Attach a Swivel Clasp

Tie off the ends with a secure knot. Attach a swivel clasp to the looped end. Your colorful lanyard is now ready for use!

Zipper Pull

Step 1: Choose Cord and Colors

Select a vibrant color for your zipper pull. Cut a shorter length, around 2 feet, as zipper pulls don't need to be too long.

Step 2: Create a Cow Hitch Knot

Fold the cord in half and pass the folded end through the zipper pull or clip. Pull the loose ends through the loop, securing the cord.

Step 3: Add Beads (Optional)

Slide colorful beads onto the two loose ends to add a decorative touch.

Step 4: Tie a Knot

Tie a secure knot at the end of the cord, ensuring that the beads are held in place.

Step 5: Attach to Zipper

Attach the looped end to the zipper of a backpack, jacket, or any item with a zipper. Now, your zipper has a personalized and vibrant pull!

Experiment with different knotting techniques, colors, and bead arrangements to create truly unique and personalized accessories. This hands-on activity enhances crafting skills and instills a sense of pride in customizing your belongings.

The Art of Macramé

Macramé is a versatile and ancient craft that involves creating intricate and decorative patterns by using knotting techniques. The art of macramé has a rich history, with its roots dating back centuries, notably flourishing during the 13th-century Arab weavers and 17th-century European sailors. In recent years, macramé has experienced a resurgence in popularity as a creative and therapeutic outlet.

Basic Macramé Knots

Square Knot

This is one of the fundamental knots that is formed by overlapping two sets of cords. It is used to create flat or spiral patterns, and it is often seen in plant hangers and wall hangings.

Half Hitch Knot

This knot is created by wrapping one cord around another. It can be used for textured and linear designs, adding depth to macramé projects.

Lark's Head Knot

The Lark's Head knot is simple, and it is commonly used to attach cords to a dowel or a ring. It serves as the starting point for many macramé projects, such as wall hangings.

Double Half Hitch Knot

This one is similar to the half hitch, but it involves two consecutive wraps around the core cord. It creates a denser and more secure knot, and it is ideal for shaping and structure.

Popular Macramé Projects

From curtains to table runners, macramé can be used to adorn various home items. Mimidellaboheme, CC BY-SA 4.0 <https://creativecommons.org/licenses/by-sa/4.0>, via Wikimedia Commons:
https://commons.wikimedia.org/wiki/File:Alberello_in_macram%C3%A9.jpg

Wall Hangings

Elaborate designs are created by combining various knots and patterns. Incorporate different materials, colors, and textures for a visually stunning result.

Plant Hangers

Utilize a combination of square knots and half hitch knots to form a cradle for holding plants. This is a stylish way to display greenery and add a bohemian touch to interiors.

Macramé Jewelry

Create intricate bracelets, necklaces, and earrings by using micro-macramé techniques. Incorporate beads and gemstones to enhance the aesthetics.

Home Décor

From curtains to table runners, macramé can be used to adorn various home items. It can be customizable to match different interior styles and color schemes.

Therapeutic Benefits of Macramé

Mindfulness and Focus

Macramé requires concentration on knotting patterns, promoting mindfulness and focus. It serves as a meditative practice, allowing individuals to be present in the creative process.

Stress Relief

Engaging in macramé provides a constructive and relaxing way to alleviate stress. The repetitive nature of knotting can have a calming effect on the mind.

Sense of Accomplishment

Completing a macramé project, whether large or intricate, instills a sense of achievement. It boosts self-esteem and encourages individuals to explore more complex patterns.

Creative Expression

Macramé allows for endless creative expression through the choice of knots, colors, and materials. Individuals can personalize their projects, resulting in unique and meaningful creations.

Whether you're a beginner or an experienced crafter, the art of macramé offers a wide range of possibilities for creating beautiful and functional items. With its therapeutic benefits and the satisfaction of producing handmade pieces, macramé continues to captivate crafters and enthusiasts worldwide.

Section 8: Tips and Tricks

Did you learn how to tie different types of knots? Great work! Now, the question remains: how fast can you tie one? Imagine you are sailing in a raft you helped build. When floating midwater, you notice two of the logs aren't tied properly, and the knots are rapidly opening up. You need to think fast and work your hands faster still. You need to re-tie the knot before the logs separate and disturb the balance of your raft.

In such a case of crisis, you don't have time to go through each knot-tying step methodically. You should think on your feet and tie the first knot that comes to mind as quickly as you can. Here are a few good tips to help you on your way to becoming a knot-tying master.

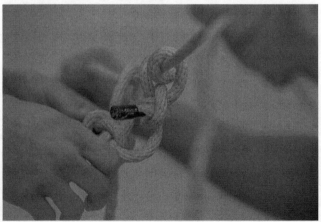

Practice tying knots.
https://commons.wikimedia.org/wiki/File:Marines_practice_knot_skills_150320-M-OD001-036.jpg

- Practice, then practice some more! Rarely is anyone a knot-tying prodigy. Once you have acquired this essential skill, you should keep practicing it until you can tie the hardest knots quickly. For instance, the fisherman's knot may take several minutes to tie the first few times. As you practice, you will find that your hands will be getting used to the motions, and your mind will be able to picture the future steps well beforehand, helping you tie faster. You can even reduce the tying time to a minute or two with enough practice.
- Practice the simple knots first. With each simple knot you tie successfully, and as fast as you can, you will develop a healthy interest in the art. By the time you reach the complicated knots (the nautical knots, in particular), you will have learned to enjoy the entire process, from understanding the motions and alignments to pulling and tightening the rope. It won't remain a chore anymore but transform into an entertaining activity.
- Prevent fraying with scotch tape. Say you need to divide a single, long coil of rope into four short lengths to pitch a tent. When you cut the rope with a pair of scissors, the resulting two ends will be frayed like Albert Einstein's hair. The knots you tie with these may not be strong enough to hold your tent. Here's a simple trick to prevent fraying.
    1. Wrap the section of the rope you want to cut with scotch tape. One to two rounds of tape will be enough.
    2. Cut with scissors from the middle of the wrap.

This way, the resulting ends will be neatly cut without any threads sticking out.

- Don't dismiss the overhand knot. In the fascinating world of knots, the most fundamental knot in the world is easy to ignore. Despite being the simplest knot to tie, it can be alarmingly difficult to untie when the tension is too high. It's not among the most secure knots either. However, as you might know by now, without the overhand knot, you cannot tie many other types of knots (like the reef knot, the fisherman's knot, the angle loop, etc.) Plus, when you need to tie a knot fast, like when your raft is failing, you can use an overhand knot and take your time to create a sturdier knot.

- Understand the pros and cons of any knot. While you can secure yourself better to a climbing harness with a double bowline, it can be dangerous if you get it wrong. A figure-eight knot is much easier and safer to tie. Go through the pros and cons of each type of knot before experimenting with it in a real-world setting.
- Carry knot-tying tools. If you haven't practiced your knots enough before heading to the great outdoors, carrying a knot-tying tool, like a Marline Spike or a specially crafted knife would be beneficial. They will speed up the process of tying many kinds of knots.

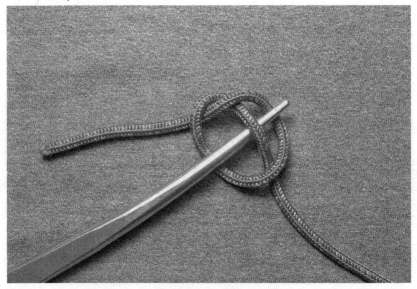

Carry knot-tying tools.
David J. Fred, CC BY-SA 2.5 <https://creativecommons.org/licenses/by-sa/2.5>, via Wikimedia Commons: https://commons.wikimedia.org/wiki/File:Marlinespike-hitch-ABOK-2030-Step3.jpg

Useful Variations and Handy Shortcuts

Tying the most complicated knots is possible with practice, but doing the same hand motions and rope inserts over and over again can become boring. That is when the following interesting variations and handy shortcuts act like a breath of fresh air. (Show each of the knots below)

Braided Square Knot

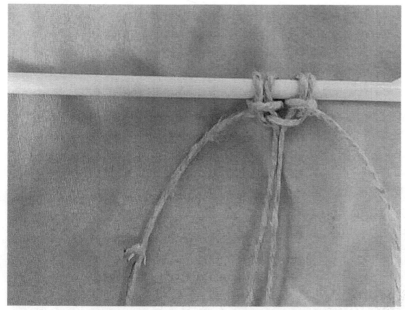

This is a fun way to practice tying a square knot.
Most Craft, CC BY 2.0 <https://creativecommons.org/licenses/by/2.0>, via Wikimedia Commons: https://commons.wikimedia.org/wiki/File:Square_(macrame_knot).jpg

This is a fun way to practice tying a square knot. At the end of this activity, you will end up with an attractive braid, just like a perfectly woven ponytail. You will need two ropes for this.

1. Tie the ropes to a rod with a Lark's Head knot (fold the rope in half, wrap it once around the rod, and insert both ends through the loop).
2. Bring them close together.
3. Hold the leftmost cord above the two middle cords and below the rightmost cord.
4. Bring the rightmost cord from under the middle cords and over (and through) the leftmost cord.
5. Pull the two ends to make a square knot that looks as if it's leaning slightly to the right.
6. Do the same, starting with the leftmost cord, then keep alternating.

You will get great practice in tying a square knot with both your hands. The more loops you complete, the better your rope braid will look.

Spiral Square Knot

Wish to transform your knots' sequence into a beautiful spiral design? For the braided knot, you alternated between the rightmost and the leftmost cords. To make a spiral out of it, you need to keep tying either a right-sided or a left-sided square knot. The more you tie, the more it will curve. If it's long enough, it will look like a spiraling strand of DNA!

Monkey's Fist

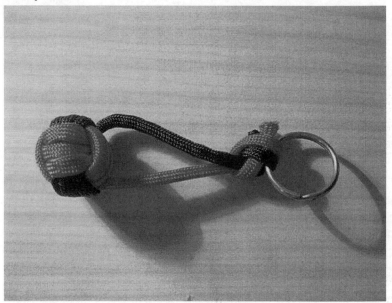

Monkey's Fist knot acts as a stopper to prevent the rope from slipping beyond the edge.
Markwell, CC BY-SA 3.0 <https://creativecommons.org/licenses/by-sa/3.0>, via Wikimedia Commons: https://commons.wikimedia.org/wiki/File:Paracord_monkey_fist.JPG

After tying your favorite knot, do those ugly little frayed ends of the rope bother you? You can cover them up with a cool, decorative knot called a Monkey's Fist. It also acts as a stopper to prevent the rope from slipping beyond the edge.

1. Wrap the rope end three times around two fingers of your left hand. Keep the fingers apart.
2. Wrap it horizontally between your fingers around the first wrapped loop.
3. Carefully pull out the structure, then insert the end through the center of the first loop and wrap it around the second loop. Do this twice more.

4. Tighten the cords by pulling the loops. The ends will emerge through the center. Put them back in to complete your Monkey's Fist.

The Bowline Shortcut

The bowline knot is one of the most useful knots in your repertoire. From anchoring boats to tying two ropes together, it has some of the best uses in the world of knot tying. However, the standard way of tying a bowline can be confusing for many. Here's a handy shortcut that will make the process easy.

1. Hold the rope in your left hand and make a loop in the middle (like turning the page of a book).
2. With your right hand, insert the top cord through the bottom of the loop. Hold it with your left hand as if to make an archway.
3. Take the rightmost end in your right hand and insert it into the archway from the left side.
4. Hold the end, along with the new loop, in your right hand and pull the alignment with both hands to tighten your bowline.

Improve your Cognitive Abilities with Exciting Activities

It is a proven theory that practicing knot-tying every day improves your cognitive abilities. Many of your cognitive skills come into action when you go through each step of tying knots.

- **Spatial Contextual Awareness:** Do you find it hard to judge the distance between two objects without using measuring tools? Do you tend to see the world in two dimensions instead of perceiving a three-dimensional space?
- **Motor Skills:** Do you find it hard to write anything? Is it tough for you to hold a pair of scissors?
- **Problem Solving:** Do you tend to come up with solutions that aren't effective? Do you make the same mistakes over and over again?
- **Memorizing:** Is it hard for you to remember simple things, like your close friend's hobbies or your mother's workplace?

All these skills will improve tenfold if you practice knot-tying regularly. The coordination between your fingers will become more refined, your memory will be as sharp as a tack, and you will start finding several effective solutions (not just one!) to your problems.

Nevertheless, is knot-tying too boring for you? Here are a few exciting activities that will keep you engaged in the art.

Knot-Tying Contest

You can play this with family or friends. Print pictures of all the finished knots shown in this book without the steps leading to them. The host will pick any picture randomly. You and the other competitors will have to recreate the knot shown. The one who finishes first will get one point. If your competitors aren't as good at knot tying as you are, then show the beginner's knots first, like the overhand and the figure-eight knots.

After playing this contest a few times, you will notice a healthy improvement in your memory and problem-solving abilities.

Friendship Bracelets

Do you want to surprise your friend with a gift or make new friends? Give them a cool, handmade friendship bracelet! You will need a 20-inch-long nylon cord – no more than two millimeters thick. You will also need to practice the sliding knot.

1. Hold the cord in a circular loop.
2. Make three smaller loops, with one end of the cord around the other end.
3. Insert the first end through the loops and tighten it.
4. Pull one end of the knot to slide a long length of the cord out (around 5 to 10 inches).
5. Tie another sliding knot on the diagonally opposite end of the first knot.

Depending on your friend's wrist, they can pull on either of the knots to loosen the bracelet or fasten it tight. If you are strapped for time, you can tie off the bracelet with a single sliding knot.

Simon Says What-Knot

This fun variation of Simon Says will test your problem-solving skills, retention, and attention span. The host will say, "Simon says...," with any type of knot. You will have to tie that knot in... say, two minutes. It will be *a miss* if you fail to tie the knot within the given time. After three misses, you will be out of the game.

If the host has only mentioned the knot without saying, "Simon says," then whoever begins to tie the knot will get a miss. Don't interrupt them just yet. Let them finish tying and see the look on their face when it's declared a miss!

Thank You

Knot tying might seem challenging at first (especially if learning new things by doing them isn't your favorite way to learn), but you've done a great job by using this book to help you! Now that you know the basic knots, you have a super cool skill you can use daily. You can turn this skill into a fun hobby, a neat craft, spice up your outdoor adventures, or just get things done faster.

Every new skill you learn makes you even more awesome. Getting good at important skills helps you be more independent, and you'll be glad for it as you grow. Remember, tying knots isn't just about making a perfect loop or twist; it's about figuring out solutions to tricky problems. Learning different knots means you're also learning to tackle tough situations.

If some knots don't work out right away, no sweat! It's all part of learning. Keep practicing; you'll be a knot-tying wizard before you know it.

Thanks for sticking with it, and congrats on finishing this book! Keep it handy for all your future knot-tying quests.

References

101 Knots. (n.d.). Decorative Knots. 101Knots. https://www.101knots.com/category/decorative-knots

101 Knots. (2017, August 4). How to Tie a Granny Knot? Tips, Variations, Uses & Video Steps. 101Knots. https://www.101knots.com/granny-knot.html

Animated Knots. (n.d.-a). Basic Knots. Www.animatedknots.com. https://www.animatedknots.com/basic-knots

Animated Knots. (n.d.-b). Half Hitch Knot. Www.animatedknots.com. https://www.animatedknots.com/half-hitch-knot

Animated Knots. (2019a). Overhand Knot. Animatedknots.com. https://www.animatedknots.com/overhand-knot

Animated Knots. (2019b, February 26). Two Half Hitches. Www.animatedknots.com. https://www.animatedknots.com/two-half-hitches-knot

Avonturier, D. van een. (2020, June 27). Essential Knots for Camping, Hiking and Survival. Dagboek van Een Avonturier. https://dagboekvaneenavonturier.com/2020/06/27/essential-knots-for-camping-hiking-and-survival/

Canyon Guides International. (n.d.). The science behind teaching & learning: Tying Knots – Canyon Guides International. Canyon Guides International. https://canyonguidesinternational.org/the-science-behind-teaching-learning-tying-knots/

Casadella, N. (2023, June 5). 13 Basic Macrame Knots: A Guide For Beginners. GANXXET. https://www.ganxxet.com/blogs/news/macrame-knots

Chest of Books. (n.d.). Decorative Knots. Chestofbooks.com. https://chestofbooks.com/crafts/camping/Creative/Decorative-Knots.html

Dave. (2019, May 6). 6 Important Knots You Should Know. Copake Camping Resort. https://copakecampingresort.com/6-important-knots-you-should-know/

Davidson, L. (2018, September 7). Useful Tips, Terms, and Techniques for Knot Tying - Grit. Www.grit.com. https://www.grit.com/tools/useful-tips-terms-techniques-knot-tying-ze0z1809zmcg/

Dean, T. (2016, May 27). How to Tie a Bow Tie: Easy Step-by-Step Video. Theknot.com. https://www.theknot.com/content/how-to-tie-a-bow-tie

Digital, P. (2022, July 22). Rope materials: a beginner's guide - RopesDirect. Ropes Direct. https://www.ropesdirect.co.uk/blog/rope-materials-a-beginners-guide-to-different-types-of-rope/

Discover Boating. (n.d.). 5 Ways to Bring Learning Onboard for the Kids This Summer. Discover Boating. https://www.discoverboating.com/resources/learning-onboard-a-boat

Flashman, J. (2021, April 21). What's the Best Tie-in Knot? The Bowline vs. The Figure 8 Knot. Climbing. https://www.climbing.com/skills/tying-in-the-bowline-vs-the-figure-8-knot/

Fouche, M. (2023, August 4). 8 Basic Survival Knots You Should Know. SkyAboveUs. https://skyaboveus.com/wilderness-survival/8-Essential-Knots-You-Should-Know-Survival-Skills

Fury, S. (n.d.). 8 Basic Knots and Their Uses. Www.survivalfitnessplan.com. https://www.survivalfitnessplan.com/blog/basic-knots-and-their-uses

Gawlikowski, G. (2016, November 9). 17 Essential Knots Every Survivalist Needs to Know. ROFFSTM. https://roffs.com/2016/11/17-essential-knots-every-survivalist-needs-know/

House, M. (2019, February 27). Six of the Most Useful Outdoor & Survival Knots You Should Know. Mountain House. https://mountainhouse.com/blogs/emergency-prep-survival/six-of-the-most-useful-outdoor-survival-knots-you-should-know

Jessyratfink. (n.d.). How to Make a Friendship Bracelet. Instructables. https://www.instructables.com/how-to-make-a-friendship-bracelet-1/

Keech, K. (2023, February 14). What Are Knots? The History and Uses. Www.theknotsmanual.com. https://www.theknotsmanual.com/knots/

Kenninger, M. (2020, February 18). History of Knots and Common Uses. Rope and Cord. https://ropeandcord.com/guides-ideas/history-of-knots-and-common-uses/

Kilpatrick, T. (2023, May 25). Securing a bundle of wood, lashing up a backpack, or just tying your shoes, the square knot is essential. The Manual. https://www.themanual.com/outdoors/how-to-tie-a-square-knot/

Knotter. (2013, July 4). Tools Used for Knotting. Solent Branch. https://igkt-solent.co.uk/knotting-tools/

Luke. (2019, February 14). A Selective History of Knots and Rope. Paracord Planet. https://www.paracordplanet.com/blog/a-selective-history-of-knots-and-rope/

Lund, T., & Garbacz, A. (2023, October 2). 4 Ways to Tie a Knot. WikiHow. https://www.wikihow.com/Tie-a-Knot

Net Knots. (n.d.-a). Bowline on a Bight - How to tie a Bowline on a Bight. Www.netknots.com. https://www.netknots.com/rope_knots/bowline-on-a-bight

Net Knots. (n.d.-b). Harness Bend Knot | How to tie a Harness Bend | All knots animated. Www.netknots.com. https://www.netknots.com/rope_knots/harness-bend

Net Knots. (n.d.-c). Slip Knot - How to tie a Slip Knot. Www.netknots.com. https://www.netknots.com/rope_knots/slip-knot

NUCC. (2022, April 12). Rigging Knots. Nucc.caves.org.au. https://nucc.caves.org.au/detailedsrt/knot/

Raleigh, D. (2022, February 15). Essential Climbing Knots – The Complete Guide. Climbing. https://www.climbing.com/skills/essential-climbing-knots-complete-guide/

Ribbins, A. (2023, August 11). Sailing Knots For Beginners Complete Guide. UKSA. https://uksa.org/sailing-knots-for-beginners-guide/

Riddle, T. C. (n.d.). Knots for Everyday Use – Texas Parks & Wildlife Department. Tpwd.texas.gov. https://tpwd.texas.gov/calendar/bentsen-rio-grande-valley/knots-for-everyday-use

Royal Museums Greenwich. (n.d.-a). How to tie a bowline knot | Royal Museums Greenwich. Www.rmg.co.uk. https://www.rmg.co.uk/stories/topics/how-tie-bowline-knot

Royal Museums Greenwich. (n.d.-b). How to tie a round turn and two half hitches knot. Www.rmg.co.uk. https://www.rmg.co.uk/stories/topics/how-tie-round-turn-two-half-hitches-knot

Royal Museums Greenwich. (n.d.-c). How to tie a sheet bend knot | Royal Museums Greenwich. Www.rmg.co.uk. https://www.rmg.co.uk/stories/topics/how-tie-sheet-bend-knot

Sailing, A. (2022, November 29). How to Tie 3 Important Sailing Knots. American Sailing. https://asa.com/news/2022/11/29/sailing-knots/

Sikora, K. (2020, April 7). Learn How to Tie Basic Fishing Knots. Www.wheredoitakethekids.com. https://www.wheredoitakethekids.com/blog/fishing-knots/

Smothermon-Short, S. (2022, March 3). 10 Knot Tying Games for Cub Scouts. Cub Scout Ideas. https://cubscoutideas.com/20457/10-knot-tying-games-for-cub-scouts/

Stearns, S. (2023, March 8). 17 Basic Macrame Knots: Step-by-Step Instructions. Sarah Maker. https://sarahmaker.com/basic-macrame-knots/

Unitarian Universalist Association. (n.d.). Activity 2: Tying Sailor Knots | Love Connects Us | Tapestry of Faith | UUA.org. Www.uua.org. https://www.uua.org/re/tapestry/children/loveconnects/session5/161791.shtml

Made in the USA
Middletown, DE
17 December 2024

6745141OR00073